1 MONTH OF
FREE
READING

at
www.ForgottenBooks.com

By purchasing this book you are eligible for one month membership to ForgottenBooks.com, giving you unlimited access to our entire collection of over 1,000,000 titles via our web site and mobile apps.

To claim your free month visit:
www.forgottenbooks.com/free894091

ISBN 978-0-265-81876-3
PIBN 10894091

Historic, archived document

Do not assume content reflects current
scientific knowledge, policies, or practices.

62.

Flowerfield's History "Since 1874"

SIXTY-FIVE YEARS AGO, John Lewis Childs established a seed and bulb business on Long Island that eventually became one of the outstanding and most reputable distributors of its time. His products were known the world over for their superior merit. The business subsequently settled in the section of Long Island known as Floral Park. In 1909, a branch of the business was established at Flowerfield, Long Island. The Flowerfield branch later became the main office and only place from which the bulb, root and seed farms of that now famous concern operated. The present ownership purchased the business at Flowerfield, lock, stock and barrel, during the early part of 1937 and started a very energetic program to maintain the business of Flowerfield at its accustomed high ranking position among the foremost growers and distributors of roots, seeds, and bulbs.

OUR GUARANTEE

Through the medium of this catalog we are inviting your patronage. Each order, small or large, will receive our immediate attention. It will be carefully filled, packed and shipped by our qualified experts. We will refill, free of charge, any order received from us in unsatisfactory condition, and in addition we will refund, without question, the full purchase price you paid if our products do not give the satisfactory results that you have the right to expect, provided, you inform us of your dissatisfaction within one year after your purchase was made.

—AND TERMS

You will probably find it more convenient to enclose your check or a money order with your purchase order. If you prefer, however, we will be very happy to open a monthly charge account for you, immediately upon receipt of your request for that service, together with the usual credit references to whom you wish us to refer.

flowerfield bulb farm, flowerfield, long Island, New York.

IRIS Kaempferi

The "Mikado" of Oriental Iris

ALTHOUGH Iris Kaempferi is one of the several species of Iris derived from Japan, it is commonly referred to as the Japanese Iris. The magnificent Iris Kaempferi, by its excellent behavior and royal appearance, serves as the model from which the quality of all other Iris from Japan can be measured. It is "Ichi Ban" meaning of the first order or No. 1 of its caste. Iris Kaempferi can be considered the Mikado of Oriental Iris whose royal regime in the Empire of the Iris has continued unchanged for centuries.

Stately Beauty June and July. During the latter part of June and all through July it reveals its glamorous stately beauty as each blossom unfurls in all its royal splendor. Massed plantings resemble the brilliant entourage of magnificently arrayed visiting royalty awaiting inspection by any who care to feast their eyes upon their Oriental charm and pompous beauty.

A Master of Loveliness—Easy to Grow. While Iris Kaempferi is undoubtedly the reigning head of the Royal Family of Iris, its cultural requirements are simple. It thrives in any rich soil, and prefers locations on the bank of a stream, brook, lake, or pond, whether a natural or artificial one. A generous feeding of manure before the young shoots appear will prove beneficial, then an occasional side dressing of a good commercial fertilizer sparingly applied during the growing season will remarkably aid the growth of your plants.

The following list of varieties have been selected from the hundreds of varieties we have to offer. It is believed that our stock represents one of the largest collections of Iris Kaempferi in this country.

Achille. Single. Very large 8-inch petals, standards purplish blue, stigmas and petals vary from deep blue to almost white. Each, 75c; 3 for $2.00; $7.50 per doz.

Amphitrite. Double. White edged, bluish violet petals, conspicuous yellow midrib, white halo. 6½ in. Each, $1.25; 3 for $3.50; $12.50 per doz.

Aoigata. Single. Dark mulberry-purple with outstanding dark veins and a halo of royal purple. Each, 75c; 3 for $2.00; $7.50 per doz.

Apollo. Single. Pure white with pink standards. An enchanting flower. Each, $1.25; 3 for $3.50; $12.50 per doz.

Aspasie. Single. Soft mauve - lavender. Each, 75c; 3 for $2.00; $7.50 per doz.

Astarte. Double. A deep hyacinth-violet. 40-inch stems, flowers 9 inches. Each, $1.00; 3 for $2.75; $10.50 per doz.

Bashu - No - Ten. Double. Gray - toned, veined with blue. 36 in. Each, $1.25; 3 for $3.50; $12.50 per doz.

Beni Chadai. Double. Vivid mahogany-purple, yellow midrib, conspicuous white halo, somewhat ruffled. Velvety; tall. Each, $2.00; 3 for $5.00; $15.00 per doz.

Betty F. Holmes. Double. One of the most gorgeous Iris. Snow-white-cream styles, lemon-yellow throat area. No garden is complete without Betty. 38 in. Each, $1.00; 3 for $2.75; $10.50 per doz.

Betty Jean Childs. Single. White, veined with splashed orchid. Tiny standards of deep purple. 33 in. Each, 75c; 3 for $2.00; $7.50 per doz.

Blue Giant. Semi-double. Truly a giant, 9 in. across. Blue with shades of violet and purple. Each, 75c; 3 for $2.00; $7.50 per doz.

Bokhara. Single. Pink tone, wavy petals, yellow central area, edged blue. Each, $1.25; 3 for $3.50; $12.50 per doz.

Introductions by Flowerfield

We recently introduced the following outstanding varieties selected from a planting of fifty thousand seedlings as worthy of their being introduced to our customers. Each one is distinctive as to color, form, and substance.

Elbrus. Single. An exceptionally large ruffled flower. Clear lavender, almost azure-blue. Moderately tall, vigorous plant. $1.50 each.

Light-in-the-Opal. Double. A gorgeous large genuine pink. Its ruffled flower is 8 in. across; of splendid substance and perfect form. Its golden throat is surrounded by a halo of blue which is outstanding in a field of clear pink. $1.50 each.

SPECIAL OFFER
One each of both varieties
only $2.50

Iris Kaempferi

Caprice. Single. Sometimes a solid lavender-blue, more often striped and mottled in an irregular way. Each, $1.25; 3 for $3.50; $12.50 per doz.

Carlton Childs. Single. Ivory-white, veined plum-wine, pink standards. Each, 75c; 3 for $2.00; $7.50 per doz.

Caroline G. Childs. Single. White, veined blue-violet, standards purple and white. 32 inch. Each, 75c; 3 for $2.00; $7.50 per doz.

Chutsai. Single. Pure mauve with snow-white style branches. 30 inch. Each, 75c; 3 for $2.00; $7.50 per doz.

Circe. Single. Very large. Dark blue-purple with short white veins and white style branches. Flower 7½ inches. Each, 75c; 3 for $2.00; $7.50 per doz.

Confucius. Single or semi-double. Red-purple splashed white with dull white-yellow midrib at base. Each, 75c; 3 for $2.00; $7.50 per doz.

Delight. Double. Dull blue, penciled with white. Each, 75c; 3 for $2.00; $7.50 per doz.

Della. Single. Light wisteria-violet. Its oriental charm is enchanting. Each, $1.00; 3 for $2.75; $10.50 per doz.

Doris Childs. Double. Pearl-white, deeply veined, rosy plum center, edged white. 32 inch. Each, 75c; 3 for $2.00; $7.50 per doz.

Red Riding Hood
75c each
3 for $2.00

Repsini
50c each
3 for $1.40

Betty F. Holmes
$1.00 each
3 for $2.75

Lilla Cox
60c each
3 for $1.50

Koki-No-Iro
A royal purple of stately beauty.
$1.25 each
3 for $3.50

flowerfield bulb farm

A Lovely Oriental Flower That Closely Rivals the Orchid

Elbrus. Single. An exceptionally large ruffled flower. Clear lavender, almost azure-blue. Moderately tall, vigorous plant. Each, $1.50.

Eleanor Parry. Double. Reddish flushed with white and blue. An exquisite flower. Each, 75c; 3 for $2.00; $7.50 per doz.

Emi Hotei. Double. Grayish white, heavily flushed and veined with blue. A gorgeous flower. Each, $1.25; 3 for $3.50; $12.50 per doz.

Fascination. Double. Pink-lavender tone, light blue tinged with pink and veined with blue. An outstanding variety. Each, $1.00; 3 for $2.75; $10.00 per doz.

Fanny Hamlet Childs. Fine violet-purple, splashed and mottled with white. 34 inches. Each, 75c; 3 for $2.00; $7.50 per doz.

Furitsuzumi. Single. A lightly splashed reddish purple of splendid form and heavy substance; petals round, drooping slightly. Each, $1.00; 3 for $2.75; $10.00 per doz.

Gekka-No-Nami. Double. Large snow-white, with ruffled petals, yellow center. A magnificent double. Each, $1.00; 3 for $2.75; $10.00 per doz.

Grace Sperling. Single. Soft violet-blue with milk-white crests. 40 inches. Each, 75c; 3 for $2.00; $7.50 per doz.

Hebe. Double. White faintly flushed with soft lavender, soft yellow-lemon throat. A rare Iris. Each, $1.75; 3 for $4.75; $17.50 per doz.

Hercule. Double. Very large petals, round, slightly waved, washed with shades of blue and purple, yellow base. Each, 75c; 3 for $2.00; $7.50 per doz.

Isabelle. Single. Very large grayish pink, small yellow spear at base, very distinct dark violet veins. A rare majestic beauty. Each, $1.00; 3 for $2.75; $10.00 per doz.

Ispahan. Single. Phlox-purple veined with white. Each, 60c; 3 for $1.75; $6.00 per doz.

Jeanette Parry. Single. White falls, veined soft blue, tiny mulberry-purple standards. Each, $1.25; 3 for $3.50; $12.50 per doz.

Kamata. Single. Dark royal-blue, velvety. A rare Iris, absolutely true to name. Each, $1.50.

Kobe. Single. Splashed reddish purple with small erect standards. Each, 75c; 3 for $2.00; $7.50 per doz.

Koki-No-Iro. Double. A large gorgeous flower. Deep purple with white styles. 14 inches. Each, $1.25; 3 for $3.50; $12.50 per doz.

Kongo San. Double. Frilled style branches and stamens. 6½-inch petals, round and frilled, royal-blue, with deep dark velvety shades of violet. A very rare Iris, imported by us a very short time ago. 42 inches. Each, $2.00.

Kumi-No-Obi. Double. Sky-blue with white at base of petals. A lovely color and an enchanting flower. Each, $1.00; 3 for $2.75; $10.00 per doz.

Kuro-Kumo. Double. Bluish purple. Style branches dark blue bordered with purple. Specially offered at $1.30 each.

La Favorite. Double. Early large white, with delicate veins of soft purple. 30 inches. Very specially priced at 60c each.

Light-in-the-Opal. Double. A gorgeous large genuine pink. Its ruffled flower is 8 inches across, of splendid substance and perfect form. Its golden throat is surrounded by a halo of blue which is outstanding in a field of clear pink. Each, $1.50.

Lilla Cox. Light blue with white veins radiating from a yellow blotch in the center. Each, 60c; 2 for $1.00.

Mahogany. Double. Deep velvety mahogany-red. A very large and conspicuously brilliant, and a strikingly handsome specimen. Each, $1.00.

Mahogany Giant. Double. Very large, deep mahogany, golden star in center, with white style branches. A pompous beauty—rarely offered. Each, $1.25; 3 for $3.50; $12.50 per doz.

Margaret S. Hendrickson. Triple. Bluish violet-veined violet, large wavy petals, white center with radiating blue coat. One of the finest and largest of the species. Each, $1.00; 3 for $2.75; $10.00 per doz.

Marjory Parry. Double. Soft mauve with a tufted center. Its stately form and soft coloring are most attractive. 36 inches. Each, 75c; 3 for $2.00.

Mrs. George Stumpp. Single. Giant white beautifully creped petals. Tiny mauve standards, styles white, flushed mauve. Each, 60c; 3 for $1.50.

Neptune. Single. Red-purple, a regal beauty. Each, 50c; 3 for $1.25; $5.00 per doz.

Nishiki Yama. Double. Large vinous mauve flushed and veined white, center of petals banded with mauve. Remarkable and rare. Specially priced at $1.25.

La Favorite Kaempferi
A study in white and veined purple

FLOWERFIELD'S Supreme Collection

One Each of the following
Five Varieties for **$4.00**

Betty F. Holmes	Elbrus
Blue Giant	La Favorite
Margaret S. Hendrickson	

Flowerfield "Approved" Bulbs are Hand Picked, Treated and Guaranteed

flowerfield, long island, New York

[5]

's *Kaempferi* ⌒All Varieties Approved by "Flowerfield"

gain new friends, we will include one un-
:d seedling with each order for Iris Kaemp-
amounting to more than $2.00.

Jo-Taki. A glamorous white stippled rose-pink. Each,

Double. Exquisite lavender-pink, with clear blue halo
nding a yellow blotch at the center. Each, 75c; 3 for

Double. An attractive plum, shading from light to
Each, 75c; 3 for $2.00; $7.50 per doz.

Lady. Single. A good white, suffused pink, giving an
l appearance of gorgeous pale pink. Each, 60c; 3 for

. Single. Amethyst-violet, yellow throat, markings
n by styles, a distinct blue flush toward center of petals.
:hes. Each, 50c; 3 for $1.25.

Double. Horizontal petals heavily veined and flushed
:ed-purple. Each, $1.00; 3 for $2.75; $10.00 per doz.

Single. Distinct blue-lavender. A rare Iris; true plants
fficult to obtain. Each, $1.00; 3 for $2.50.

. Double plus. Deep blue-purple, with white styles
ellow throat markings. Each, $1.00; 3 for $2.50.

ing Hood. Single. Amaranth-red, veined white. Each,

. Double. Light blue with white veins. Each, 50c;
$1.40; $5.00 per doz.

Rose Anna. Double. Gray with deep red-purple veins, shading darker around yellow zone. Each, $1.00.

Salammbo. Double. Rose-red with darker veins; truly a beautiful red Iris. Each, $1.25; 3 for $3.50.

Shishi Ikari. Triple. A vivid claret-red. 36 inches. Each,
$1.00; 3 for $2.75.

Subotai. Single. Fine rose-red with blue zone circling yellow
center. One of the rarest Iris. 34 inches. Each, $2.00.

Suibijin. Single. Red-purple with light veins. Outstanding
in its royal pompous colorings. Each, 75c; 3 for $2.50.

Taiheiraku. Double. Brilliant purple with light veins. Each,
75c.

Temple Flower. Single. Bluish violet with white edges. Each,
50c; 3 for $1.35; $5.00 per doz.

Totty's True Blue. Double. A splendid dark violet-blue.
Each, 50c.

Violet Beauty. Single. Velvety pansy-violet. Each, 60c;
$5.00 per doz.

Violet Giant. Double. Reddish purple, dark veins; one of
the very largest ever introduced. Each, $2.00; $20.00
per doz.

White Giant. Double. A pure white of great size and substance. A gorgeous large flower. The Mikado of the
white Irises. Each, $1.50; $15.00 per doz.

Yama Yama. Single. White crinkled, flushed lavender,
with standards of bright soft violet. 30 inches. Each,
60c; 3 for $1.60; $6.00 per doz.

Zephyr. Double. A magnificent white flushed with lavender of light blue. A rare beauty. Each, $1.00; $10.00
per doz.

Japanese Iris
blending of pastel shades and tints, indescribable and
lovely beyond words

Iris Seedlings

The exciting glorious thrill of producing a new
flower—unnamed—perhaps unusual—distinct and
outstanding as to color, form and structure, can be
yours by planting Iris seedlings — never before
seen in flower — may be rare! — may be valuable!

IRIS SEEDLINGS Unnamed, Each
A Dozen at $1.75 **25¢**

flowerfield bulb farm

Tall Bearded Iris

GROWN AT FLOWERFIELD

There are so many varieties of Tall Bearded Iris offered that it becomes confusing to one who endeavors to make a selection from the long general lists. In an attempt to be of assistance to our customers, we have selected the following as a choice cross section of all the varieties available. Each one has been grown here at Flowerfield; some are comparatively new varieties, some are older ones, however, all have been tried and found very satisfactory.

Cultural Directions

The cultural requirements are simple for this Iris. The plants can be grown in any average well-drained sweet soil in a sunny location where the plants will be assured all the sunshine possible. Bonemeal has been proven a satisfactory fertilizer. Manures can be used in rotted form, only if well spaded under so that no humus will come in contact with the rhizomes. It has been found that the best time to plant this Iris is from midsummer to the last part of September, so that the roots will become well established before freezing. We prefer to plant during July and August.

If the soil appears dry at planting time, thoroughly soak the dug-up area to be planted, spread the roots over the moist surface, and replace the soil over them. The rhizome should be just below the surface with the soil tamped down around it, so that it is firmly held in position by the packed soil.

Blue Monarch. A clear violet-blue self, with large flowers on tall stems. Each, 75c.

Blue Triumph. A tall clear pale ice-blue having a smooth velvety finish. An Iris of great dignity; one of the finest blues. 40 inches. Each, $1.50.

Blue Velvet. A very beautiful flower, deep blue-violet. Well branched, big blooms. 30 inches. Each, 35c.

Cinnabar. Standards violet-purple. Falls, flaring, cotinga-purple. General effect is a rich dark red of one tone. 42 inches. Each, 35c.

Clara Noyes. An unusual new variety with colors blended much as in a Talisman Rose. Low growing. Standards are tan, flushed heliotrope, falls reddish bronze. Yellow beard and haft, undertone of the same color. Each, 50c.

Crystal Beauty. New large pure white, tall and well-branched stalk. Each, $1.25.

Desert Dawn. A glorious rich yellow and lavender blend. Beautiful and large. Each, 50c.

Eros. Considered the pinkest Iris, with warm yellow haft and beard, giving a definite effect of salmon-pink. 36 inches. Each, $1.00.

Ethelwyn Dubuar. A new very large pink. Each, 50c.

Frivolite. A very fine French origination, medium size blooms. A beautiful shade of lavender-pink. 48 inches. Each, $1.00.

Gleam. Very large, luminous, pale blue self, nearly a true blue. Brilliant orange beard. Lasting substance. 48 inches. Each, 50c.

Indian Chief. Most popular new Iris. Velvety falls are deep blood-red blended with bronze, and the standards are considerably lighter in tone. Large, tall, and well branched. 32 inches. Each, 35c.

King Juba. Big and bold, with yellow standards and falls of Indian Lake. Medium. Each, 50c.

King Midas. Bright bronze-toned Iris. Standards, golden buff; falls, iridescent garnet-brown, lighted by orange beard and golden haft. 24 inches. Each, 50c.

Mme. Serouge. Very beautiful free-flowering Iris of great size and vigorous growth. A clear deep violet-blue self. 30 inches. Each, 60c.

Omaha. Combination of coppery pink and brownish cinnamon. Each, 35c.

Pink Opal. Tallest of lavender-pinks. Blooms are large and softly colored. 48 inches. Each, 50c.

Selene. Extra large, pure white, of thick substance. A giant. Each, 35c.

Snow White. A very pure white, but markings are pale green which gives it a fragile appearance. 36 inches. Each, 35c.

Trail's End. Standards, yellow overlaid orange-red. Each, $1.50.

William Mohr. Most orchid-like of all Iris. Ground color is pale lilac flushed darker, veined manganese-violet, large flower. Each, 50c.

Tall Bearded Iris

Siberian Iris

These Iris are tall with slender stems and narrow, grasslike foliage. They are among the best for cut flowers. The plants do well in a moist location as well as in any good garden location.

The following varieties are offered at:

Each, 25c; 3 for 60c; $2.25 per doz.

Bob White. Pure white.

Butterfly. Soft medium blue.

Duchess of York. Deep violet-blue.

Emperor. True dark violet.

Florrie Riddler. Dark showy blue.

Kingfisher Blue. Very bright sky-blue.

Lady Northcliffe. Rich violet.

Mrs. Rowe. Lavender-pink.

Paillon. Gleaming light blue.

Peggy Perry. Rich dark blue.

Periwinkle. Violet-blue, turquoise midrib.

Perry's Blue. Almost sky-blue.

Pigmy. Low dark violet.

Skylark. Lovely blue edged white.

Snow Queen. Low white.

Stardust. Tall white, with yellow throat.

Sunnybrook. Low medium blue.

Thelma. Alice blue with white.

True Blue. Almost real blue.

White Dove. White, very tall.

Hemerocallis ～ A New Family of Super-Size "Day Lilies" or "Lemon Lil

In recent years tremendous improvement has been made through hybridization in the Day Lilies erocallis). As a result varieties are now available which afford a marvelous range of color from palest to deep bronze and orange-red. These new erocallis with their lovely coloring will give ennial plantings that enrichment of tone tha much desired. Best of all, these plants are pe hardy, display strong resistance to droug heat, and their clumps increase in size and st each year without requiring frequent dividi replanting.

Hemerocallis Collection

Colors, deep yellow, orange to coppery red, glistening yellow, and apricot-yellow.

3 plants Bay State. Deep yellow.
3 plants George Yeld. Orange to copper-red.
3 plants Mrs. W. H. Wyman. Yellow.
3 plants Sir Michael Foster. Apricot-yellow.

12 Plants, Only $3.90

Bay State. Deep yellow flowers of mediu bloom during late June and early July.
3 feet. Each, 35c; 3 for $1.00; $3.50 per

Cinnabar. Orange to coppery red blending t with yellow throat. Blooms in mid-June, ing 3½ feet high. Each, 70c; 3 for $2.00; per doz.

D. D. Wyman. Large flowers of orange-yello superimposed on bronze-red. Blooms in Ju July. Each, 50c; 3 for $1.40; $5.00 per do

George Yeld. Outer petals colored with rich orange, inner petals blend towards orange-bronze. Blooms June and July, growing 3½ high. Each, 50c; 3 for $1.40; per doz.

Golden Dream. Flowers have wide ' of deep gold, and bloom in June July. Each, 45c; 3 for $1.25; $4.5 doz.

Goldeni. Deep gold flowers bloom d June and July. Height 3 feet. Each 3 for $1.00; $3.50 per doz.

J. A. Crawford. A tall plant, growing 3 feet high, with clear golden rec' petals. Blooms during June and Each, 35c; 3 for $1.00; $3.50 per c

Lemona. Wide petals of a lemon-yellow Blooms during June and July, growing 3 high. Each, 35c; 3 for $1.00; $3.50 per dc

Mrs. W. H. Wyman. Pale glistening yellov flowers blooming in July and August. H 3½ feet. Each, 35c; 3 for $1.00; $3.50 pei

Ophir. Free-blooming golden yellow flowers b ing during June and July. Height 4 feet. 50c; 3 for $1.40; $5.00 per doz.

Sir Michael Foster. Apricot-yellow flowers, pet shaped. Blooms during June and July, ing up stately spikes 3½ feet high. Each 3 for $1.00; $3.50 per doz.

New Hemerocallis, Mrs. W. H. Wyman, 35c each

flowerfield bulb f

Korean Chrysanthemums

Provide a Wealth of Color in the Autumn When Other Flowers Are Gone

The recently introduced Korean Hybrid Chrysanthemums which bloom from late September until heavy frost, bring to a glorious climax the season of color in the garden. When other flowers begin to fade, these plants burst forth with an indescribably brilliant display of colors made all the more striking because of the absence of other flowers when the cool fall season advances.

Among the many merits of the newer Korean Hybrids is the increased hardiness over the older classes of Chrysanthemums. The flowers are excellent for cutting and are borne on graceful and yet vigorous plants growing between two to four feet high. The wonderful range of colors and diversified forms of the flowers make them one of the most desirable additions to every garden.

Hebe—a fine single variety

FOUR POPULAR VARIETIES
Moderately Priced

Ceres. Soft buff-yellow blending to coppery bronze.
Daphne. Golden rose with a glint of lilac-rose.
Diana. Delicate rose-pink, triple-ray petals tinted with lilac-rose.
Mars. Velvety crimson, blending to wine-red.
Any of the above varieties: Each 25c; 3 for 70c; $2.50 per doz.
SPECIAL COLLECTION: One of each above, 4 plants, for 80c.

One of the Newest and Best Chrysanthemums

Jane Kelsey. A fine clear pink, single flower excellent for cutting. Blooms in October and early November. Height 2 to 3 feet. Each $1.00; 3 for $2.50; $10.00 per doz.

Two Early Double Hybrids

Romany. Carmine and nopal red. A perfect flower of excellent form and breath-taking brilliance.
The Moor. Amaranth-purple, or port-wine-red. Unusual shade.
The above varieties: Each 50c; 3 for $1.25; $5.00 per doz.

Korean Chrysanthemums Recently Introduced

Ember. A warm glowing bronze. Each 75c; 3 for $2.00; $7.50 per doz.
Hebe. Lavender-pink flowers with a faint shimmering halo. About 3 inches across. Each 30c; 3 for 85c; $3.00 per doz.
Indian Summer, Double. Vivid glowing orange flower which is extremely frost-resistant and sturdy. One of the best varieties. Each 45c; 3 for $1.25; $4.50 per doz.
King Midas, a 1937 Double introduction. Soft yellow-bronze, tinted, double. Flowers measuring 4 inches across. Height 2½ feet. Blooms in late September. Each 65c; 3 for $1.75; $6.50 per doz.
Orion. Compact brilliant yellow flower especially suited for cutting. Each 30c; 3 for 85c; $3.00 per doz.
Vulcan. Garnet-crimson, shading to carmine and bronze. An unusually rich-toned flower. Each 65c; 3 for $1.75; $6.50 per doz.

A Complete Korean Hybrid Chrysanthemum Collection

Twelve outstanding varieties, including the sensational Jane Kelsey. A marvelous range of colors and diversity of flower forms.

Twelve Plants for Only $4.00
(Regular value $5.50)

Inexpensive Collection of Mixed Colors
Three Chrysathemums for 60c; $1.85 per doz.

flowerfield, long island, New York

Ember—very luminous, orange-bronze color

King Midas—flowers measure 4 inches across

Flowerfield's Superior Gladiolus

Long Island Grown—Known for Their Superior Merit

The modern Gladiolus combines more outstanding qualities than any other flower now in modern culture.

The Gladiolus is adaptable to a variety of soil and climatic conditions and can be planted from late April to late June in any well-spaded moderately good soil that has a sunny location.

The Gladiolus corms offered by us are carefully protected from thrip and disease. We use the very latest and most modern treatments to insure their superior quality. Our sterilization methods include the use of a new fumigating chamber in which all our corms receive cyanide gas fumigations. These gas treatments are repeated at ten-day intervals until every corm has been fumigated 3 times.

After we had thoroughly checked, compared, and tried the latest introductions, as well as the popular favorites, we selected the following list which we believe covers all the colors obtainable. The list includes those varieties which will produce the finest exhibition spikes, and the graceful primulinus types. In order that our selections would assure complete satisfaction to even the inexperienced gardener, we only selected those varieties which we have found to be reliable and easily grown.

The corms offered are all first size and measure 1½ inches in diameter and up. We can also supply corms measuring from 1¼ inches to 1½ inches in diameter at 20 per cent less than the prices listed, to anyone who prefers the smaller size.

GLADIOLUS VARIETIES

AFLAME. A fine variety for exhibition as well as the garden. Begonia-rose, blending to orange-red near the edges. Three for 25c; 75c per doz; $5.00 per 100.

ALBATROS. One of the very finest pure whites for exhibition purposes. 6 to 8 florets open at a time. Three, 35c; $1.00 per doz.; $7.00 per 100.

ALBINO. A pure glistening white. Florets open wide, 4-5 inches in diameter. Three for 20c; 60c per doz.; $4.00 per 100.

AMADOR. A sparkling and glistening red with stately spikes bearing 5 to 8 large florets. Three for 25c; 75c per doz.; $5.00 per 100.

APRICOT GLOW. Rich and warm apricot shade. The flowers are large, widely opened and well placed on the strong, vigorous spike. Three for 15c; 50c per doz.; $3.00 per 100.

AVE MARIA. Truly a flower of perfect form. The blooms, carried 6 to 8 on the well proportioned stalk, are an exquisite light blue with a touch of purple. Three for 25c; 75c per doz.; $5.00 per 100.

BAGDAD. A vigorous grower, well suited for exhibition work. The flowers are colored a smoky old rose, with shadings of begonia-rose. Three for 25c; $5.00 per 100.

BEACON. Bright rose-scarlet with large cream blotch. Blooms are large and waved. Spikes are very tall and straight, opening many florets. Each, 30c; three for 80c; $3.00 per doz.

BERTY SNOW. Lovely lavender-pink flowers, flecked with darker hue. Fine substance and well proportioned. Three for 15c; 50c per doz.; $3.25 per 100.

BETTY NUTHALL. An outstanding variety of warm coral-pink, shading to orange with a yellow marked throat. This large graceful flower is excellent for exhibitions. Three for 20c; 60c per doz.; $4.00 per 100.

BILL SOWDEN. Immense deep red flowers, with dark red flecks. Many rate this as the finest red gladiolus. Three for 30c; 90c per doz.; $6.00 per 100.

BLEEDING HEART. One of the better blotched varieties, being white, tinged with pink and having a large red blotch. The spike is tall and straight, and the placement of the florets is perfect. Three for 30c; 90c per doz.; $6.00 per 100.

BLUE DANUBE. Exquisitely true amethyst-blue with a fine dark blotch, giving a lovely melding of dark hues. With a tall, well-proportioned spike, it is an excellent exhibition variety. Three for 50c; $1.50 per doz.; $10.00 per 100.

CHARLES DICKENS. A popular favorite of violet-purple, on an exceptionally tall and strong spike. Certainly the best purple gladiolus and at a modest price. Three for 15c; 50c per doz.; $3.00 per 100.

COMMANDER KOEHL. A delightful bright blood-red, of magnificent size and form. It is outstanding as a cut flower for exhibition purposes, and is moderately priced. Three for 30c; 90c per doz.; $6.00 per 100.

COPPER-BRONZE. Deep salmon-bronze with copper-like gleam. A stately cut flower variety. Three for 25c; 75c per doz.; $5.00 per 100.

CORYPHEE. Unusual in its purity of hue; a clear pink. 8 to 10 florets open at a time on strong tall stems. Three for 40c; $1.25 per doz.; $9.00 per 100.

Colored "Glad" spikes by the armful at "Flowerfield."

Individual hand work always plays an important part in producing "Quality" at "Flowerfield."

Harry Dare — For twenty years an enthusiastic "Glad" expert at "Flowerfield."

flowerfield bulb farm

Gladiolus ～ New and Reliable Varieties

DEBONAIR. A gladiolus aristocrat. Deep and warm La France pink with creamy throat markings, and darker pink flecks. Exceptionally strong and tall grower. Three for 25c; 75c per doz.; $5.00 per 100.

DR. F. E. BENNETT. Dark peach-red with flaming red superimposed. Speckled ruby and creamy white. The firm flowers are well placed on a tall stem. Three for 25c; 75c per doz.; $5.00 per 100.

DUNA. A tea rose delicate salmon-buff, shading to light creamy yellow. The color effect is unusual. The spikes are well balanced and of medium height. Three for 30c; 90c per doz.; $6.00 per 100.

FRANK J. McCOY. An exhibition variety, having large rose to pink florets with scarlet blotch. Tall and stately. Three for 30c; 90c per doz.; $6.00 per 100.

GATE OF HEAVEN. A good yellow is bound to meet with popular enthusiasm. This variety is outstanding. Beautifully ruffled, clear and deep yellow. Three for 70c; $2.25 per doz.; $16.00 per 100.

GIANT NYMPH. A light rose-pink with creamy yellow throat. A beautiful gladiolus, yet one of the lowest in price. Three for 20c; 60c per doz.; $4.00 per 100.

GLORIANA. A pleasing salmon shaded with gold. The tall and erect stems proudly carry many fine, well opened blooms. Three for 15c; 50c per doz.; $3.00 per 100.

GOLDEN CHIMES. Pure soft yellow, nicely ruffled flowers, symmetrically placed on straight spikes. Three for 65c; $2.15 per doz.; $15.50 per 100.

GOLDEN DREAM. Clear golden yellow of very distinctive appearance. Tall spikes with many flowers opened at a time. Three for 15c; 55c per doz.; $3.50 per 100.

HALLEY. An early blooming, delicate salmon-pink variety. A beautiful Gladiolus at moderate cost. Three for 20c; 60c per doz.; $4.25 per 100.

KING ARTHUR. A ruffled gladiolus colored deep lavender. The large ruffled blooms make an unusually fine show. Three for 20c; 60c per doz.; $4.00 per 100.

LA PALOMA. A clear orange variety of firm substance. Having an unusual hue, it is one of the most popular orange shaded gladiolus. Three for 15c; 50c per doz.; $3.00 per 100.

LOS ANGELES. Shrimp-pink with orange blotch and carmine throat. It is an unusual and valuable variety because each corm produces, in succession, several spikes of flowers. Three for 15c; 55c per doz.; $3.50 per 100.

LOYALTY. Deep rich yellow. Late bloomer. Three for 20c; 60c per doz.; $4.00 per 100.

MAID OF ORLEANS. Pure white with a creamy throat. Perfectly formed, and excellent for cutting. Three for 25c; 75c per doz.; $5.00 per 100.

MAMMOTH WHITE. An enormous pure white flower measuring as much as 7 inches across. This giant exhibition gladiolus often stands 5 feet high. Three for 30c; 90c per doz.; $6.00 per 100.

MARMORA. An exhibition variety of immense size and unusual coloring. Lavender-gray with purplish blotched florets on a stately spike. Three for 30c; 90c per doz.; $6.00 per 100.

MARY ELIZABETH. Beautiful ruffled shade, delicate yellow in throat. Eight or more florets open at one time. A late bloomer. Three for 15c; 50c per doz.; $3.50 per 100.

MILDRED LOUISE. Definitely an unusual and outstanding variety. Soft pink, strawberry hued, melting into orange-yellow in the throat. Faint bluish traces enhance the coloring. Three for 50c; $1.50 per doz.; $10.00 per 100.

MINUET. The standard of comparison of all lavender gladiolus. This variety is beautifully pure and light in its lavender hue. The flowers are large and of firm texture. Three for 30c; 90c per doz.; $6.00 per 100.

MISS ALAMEDA. Deep salmon-pink blended with a carmine blotch. Florets are large and many open at once on long, graceful spikes. Early bloomer. Three for 15c; 50c per doz.; $3.50 per 100.

MISS NEW ZEALAND. A giant New Zealand variety. Florets measure as much as 8 inches in diameter, and open six or more on a long spike with many buds. Flower head is very heavy and splendid for exhibition or home garden. Each, 20c; three for 50c; $2.00 per doz.

MOTHER MACHREE. Smoky lavender, tinted with salmon; difficult to describe, but never forgotten when seen in its real beauty. Tall strong stems. Three for 30c; 95c per doz.; $6.50 per 100.

W. H. PHIPPS. Long spikes of 15 to 20 salmon-rose florets open at one time. This late blooming exhibition flower has long enjoyed popularity. Three for 20c; 65c per doz.; $4.50 per 100.

MRS. FRANK PENDLETON. A beautiful and yet inexpensive gladiolus. Salmon-pink, maroon blotch. Three for 20c; 65c per doz.; $4.50 per 100.

MRS. P. W. SISSON. A very lovely cameo-pink, slightly ruffled. Large florets on a tall spike. Three for 20c; 65c per doz.; $4.50 per 100.

ORANGE QUEEN. A better primulinus grandiflorus variety, having a lovely light orange color, deepening at edges of petals. Many florets carried on dainty spikes. Three for 15c; 50c per doz.; $3.25 per 100.

PELEGRINA. Distinctly dark in hue, this early exhibition and decorative gladiolus is colored a deep violet-blue. Three for 35c; $1.00 per doz.; $7.00 per 100.

PFITZER'S TRIUMPH. Salmon to bright orange-red. The florets are large, wide open, and perfectly placed. A gorgeous variety. Three for 25c; 75c per doz.; $5.50 per 100.

PHYLLIS McQUISTON. A beautiful glowing shrimp-pink, rather deep in hue. White throat is slightly marked with rose. The flowers hold up well after cutting. Three for 25c; 75c per doz.; $5.50 per 100.

PICARDY. This variety has become synonymous with the word gladiolus. This sensational shrimp-pink flower has met with universal acclaim. No garden complete without it. Three for 20c; 60c per doz.; $4.00 for 100.

RED LORY. Carmine-rose-colored, with purplish blotches. Almost the entire spike opens at once. Three for 35c; $1.15 per doz.; $8.00 per 100.

RED PHIPPS. Glowing red florets, on a tall firm stem. A striking variety for exhibition purposes. Three for 35c; $1.00 per doz.; $7.00 per 100.

SALBACH'S PINK. Lavender-pink, with soft carmine lip in the throat. The flowers are large and wide open and of firm substance. Three for 35c; $1.00 per doz.; $7.50 per 100.

SMILING MAESTRO. Deep salmon-rose, flecked with darker rose. Outstanding for its warm, rich color, and unusually large flowers open ten to twelve at a time. Three for 50c; $1.50 per doz.; $10.00 per 100.

SONATINE. Light clear pink, with small red blotch. Tall and strong exhibition spikes carry seven to eight 6-inch flowers. Three for 25c; 75c per doz.; $5.00 per 100.

STAR OF BETHLEHEM. Exceptionally good white, with a delicate cream shading in throat. Tall and vigorous grower and an excellent cut flower. Three for 25c; 85c per doz.; $6.00 per 100.

VAGABOND PRINCE. A gladiolus in the mahogany shade. Garnet-brown with a small blotch of flame-scarlet. Eight to ten well placed florets open at once. Distinctive variety. Each, 25c; three for 65c; $2.50 per doz.

WASAGA. A ruffled glowing buff variety, clear throat, with no flecks or markings. Three for 25c; 75c per doz.; $5.00 per 100.

WURTEMBERGIA. Brilliant red, with white throat. Unusual and dazzling variety, attractive anywhere. Three for 30c; 90c per doz.; $6.00 per 100.

A MODERN FUMIGATING CHAMBER. All our Gladiolus bulbs are scientifically treated in this chamber, as a guarantee against thrip and other insect pests.

Millions of bulbs are "racked off" in our temperature-controlled storage warehouse to protect the life and vitality of every flower bulb.

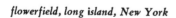

flowerfield, long island, New York

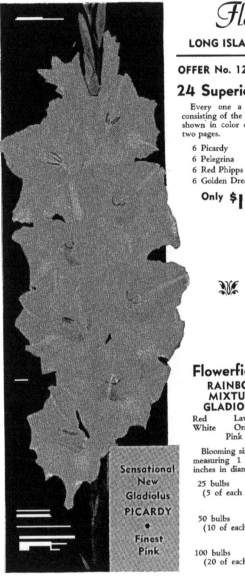

Flowerfield's Finest

LONG ISLAND GROWN

OFFER No. 120

24 Superior Gladiolus

Every one a winner, consisting of the varieties shown in color on these two pages.

6 Picardy
6 Pelegrina
6 Red Phipps
6 Golden Dream

Only $1.55

Flowerfield's
RAINBOW MIXTURE GLADIOLUS

Red   Lavender
White   Orange
      Pink

Blooming size bulbs, measuring 1 to 1½ inches in diameter.

25 bulbs
(5 of each color)
40c

50 bulbs
(10 of each color)
70c

100 bulbs
(20 of each color)
$1.25

Sensational
New
Gladiolus
PICARDY
•
Finest
Pink

Pelegrina

flowerfield bulb farm

[12]

Exhibition Gladiolus

KNOWN FOR THEIR SUPERIOR QUALITY

SPECIAL GLADIOLUS
Collection

NAMED VARIETIES
Your Own Selection
of the Following:
Aflame
Albatros
Charles Dickens
Dr. F. E. Bennett
Giant Nymph
Marmora
Picardy
Orange Queen
Pfitzer's Triumph
Wasaga

25 bulbs
(5 each of 5 varieties)
$1.25

50 bulbs
(10 each of 5 varieties)
$2.00

100 bulbs
(10 each of 10 varieties)
$3.50

Flowerfield's
FINEST EXHIBITION
MIXTURE

A chromatically balanced blend
of the best named varieties; each
bulb producing a large flower
spike, perfect in form and super-
latively colored.

The Finest Gladiolus Mixture
(No. 1 size corms)

dozen	....	$ 0.50
100	....	3.00
1000	....	25.00

Red Phipps

Golden Dream

flowerfield, long island, New York

Amaryllis Hippeastrum

The Amaryllis, often termed the queen of all bulbous flowers, is one of the most beautiful and interesting of all garden subjects. The species is closely related to the lily family, and from the large number of varieties available, we have chosen those Amaryllis which will appeal to the gardener for their beauty and ease of culture.

GIANT AMERICAN HYBRIDS

A fine giant-flowering strain of Amaryllis with 4 to 6 enormous and perfectly shaped blooms on each stalk. Available in a beautiful range of colors. Each, 50c; three for $1.40; $5.00 per doz.

BELLADONNA LILY

An old favorite, having satiny white flowers with a tinge of pink. The plant is hardy, but prefers a dry location in rich sandy loam with a covering of leaves during the winter. Extra strong bulbs, each, 50c; three for $1.40; $5.00 per doz.

AMARYLLIS HALLI

(Lycoris Squamigera)

A scarce and hardy variety which each year sends up tall flower scapes crowned with a cluster of large blossoms. The attractive foliage grows in early spring and dies down, to be mysteriously followed in August by the appearance of flower stalks attaining a height of two or three feet. The lily-like flowers, clustered 8 to 12 to a stalk, are lavender, tinted pink, fragrant and exceedingly beautiful. Fine bulbs, perfectly hardy anywhere without protection. $1.00 each; three for $2.80; $10.00 per doz.

The Ever Popular

BLEEDING HEART

(Dicentra Spectabilis)

An old-fashioned summer-flowering perennial having long slender racemes of graceful pink heart-shaped flowers which bloom in early spring. The foliage is especially attractive, and will provide masses of green to enhance the beauty of the garden until late in summer. Finest field-grown clumps: Each, 50c; three for $1.40; $5.00 per doz.

Bleeding Heart

flowerfield bulb farm

he Feathery **ASTILBE**

(Spirea, Arendsi Hybrids)

ry showy and attractive perennial herbs bearing a mass of feathery
r heads in June and July. They serve particularly well in providing
ng masses of bloom during early summer. Plants grow 2 feet high,
asy to grow, and succeed best in half-shaded position in any good,
garden soil.

ng healthy plants of any of the following:
Each, 50c; three for $1.25; $5.00 per doz.

Spirea, Gloria Superba

ica. Feathery lilac-pink.
hyst. Deep violet · purple.
wers on branched spikes.
  Cuperus. Long, drooping
re white spikes.
at. Deep crimson.
a **Superba.** Deep rose-pink,
e of the best.

Kriemhilde. Delicate salmon-rose.
Peach Blossom. Peach-pink; good
  for forcing.
Pink Pearl. Compact spikes of delicate pink.
Queen Alexandra. Deep peach-
  pink hue.
Rhineland. A bright red, shading
  to crimson and salmon.

Collection of 10 Astilbes

One of each of the above varieties $**4**.25

---

ummer-Flowering Oxalis Or Lucky Four-Leaf Clover

. lucky four-leaf clover for your garden or for in-
r pot culture. Legend says these rapid growing
·s "bring luck to the garden in which they grow,
·ell as to the person who grows them."

rom the practical standpoint, no bulb is so valuable
edging the borders of walks or flower beds as the
.ty summer-flowering Oxalis. When planted two or

three inches apart, they produce an unbroken row of
elegant four-leaved foliage and pretty pink and white
flowers. Best of all, they grow profusely and bloom
quickly after planting, thereby furnishing a neat and
attractive border the whole season long. They are also
splendid when planted in a mass, and make a very
showy bed.

Summer-Flowering Oxalis

Cultivation

Plant the bulbs about 2 or 3 inches apart, just be-
neath the surface of the ground. The bulbs grow
remarkably well under almost all conditions. Although they can withstand a great deal of sun, some
watering is advisable.

For indoor culture, a very attractive arrangement
is to place three bulbs in a triangle, just below the
soil surface, in each pot.

We offer three of the finest varieties of Oxalis
which we grow at Flowerfield, Long Island:

Shamrock. Finest four-leaf clover, pink flower. 35c
per doz. $2.00 per 100.

Lasiandra. Four-leaf clover, pink flower. 25c per
doz.; $1.50 per 100.

Deppei. Three-leaf clover, white flower. 20c per
doz.; $1.25 per 100.

Tuberous-Rooted Begonias

Easily Cultivated — Popular as pot plants and for bedding out-of-doors

The tuberous-rooted Begonias, which are becoming more popular every year, both as pot plants and for bedding out-of-doors, are the result of crossing several species that differed considerably in habit. They are easily cultivated. For bedding out in partial shade, these plants have no equals. They rival the gloxinia as a window or conservatory plant, and the enormous size and intense brilliance of the flowers astonish those who have never seen any but the ordinary house Be-

gonia. They are excellent for semi-shady locations, and are therefore, especially adaptable to the shaded city garden.

The root can be started from March to June and will soon be in full bloom. They may be started at intervals, having an earlier and later lot. Have the bed heavily manured and the soil level with the surface of the surrounding ground, as the roots run near the top. Frequent watering is needed to keep the top of the bed constantly moist. Plant about a foot apart.

SINGLE FLOWERING TYPE

Either frilled or plain edged offered in six beautiful colors.

Orange	Rose	White
Pink	Scarlet	Yellow

Any color, your selection, each, 25c; three for 70c; $2.50 per doz.

Mixed colors, our selection, six for $1.25; $2.25 per doz.

SINGLE CRESTED TYPE

During the past few years this type has been highly improved; its dwarf stocky growth with masses of flowers makes it suitable for both bedding and show purposes.

COLORS

Yellow	Dark red	Rose shades	Salmon shades

Your selection of colors, each 25c; three for 70c; $2.50 per doz.

Mixed colors, our selection, six for $1.25; $2.25 per doz.

DOUBLE FRILLED OR CARNATION TYPE

This glorious flower is now available in its enormously improved form.

COLORS

SOLID	VARIABLE
White	Rose
Yellow	Apricot
Dark red	Dark Salmon

You select the colors you desire. Each, 30c; three for 85c; $3.00 per doz.
Mixed colors of our selection. Six for $1.50; $2.75 per doz.

flowerfield bulb farm

Peonies ～ HERBACEOUS

Outstanding Decorative Qualities. An ancient Chinese flower of exquisite beauty. Legend says it was named after the mythical physician, Paeon. In an endeavor to trace its origin, one will find it mentioned in the early writings of the Greeks and Romans, who believed the Peony roots possessed a curative power. Centuries ago the Chinese grew Peonies for their glorious decorative qualities. At that time the Chinese were considered one of the most cultured races in the Far East.

A new Wealth of Color and Size. Credit for the development of the Peony to its modern state belongs, first, to the great gardeners of France, who, during the eighteenth and nineteenth centuries, by their botanical genius, developed the modern, richly colored, fragrant, double Peony of today; second, credit to no small extent, belongs to our own American originators, who during the past century have introduced many new Peonies, which possess a wealth of color, elegance and charm never dreamed of by our European and Far Eastern brothers of centuries ago.

Hardy and Easy to Grow. Peonies are now considered one of the most hardy and easily grown of all garden flowers, and can be planted from September until the ground freezes; most growers, however, prefer to plant during September or early October. They withstand severe cold winters, and thrive much better in localities where the climatic conditions bring, at the very least, a heavy frost. Their soil requirements are modest; they do well in all kinds, but do best in a deep, rather moist loam, with a clay subsoil. In practice, it has been found that its root should be planted in well spaded soil, with the eyes toward the surface, with not more than two inches of soil covering the topmost eyes.

Fertilizing. Peonies are very heavy feeders and require some fertilizing. It is impossible to say how much should be applied to your soil; we would suggest using bonemeal at the time the root is set, and in the spring, apply commercial fertilizer to each plant, remembering that commercial fertilizers are highly concentrated, and should be used sparingly.

The following is a list of Peonies that are grown here at Flowerfield, and is made up of the varieties which, in our opinion, are the very best for color selection, growth of plant, and keeping quality of the bloom.

RATING AS DESIGNATED BY AMERICAN PEONY SOCIETY
The rating shown at the left side of each variety listed has been established by the American Peony Society. Each variety has been rated for excellence by them on a scale of 10. Nevertheless, many varieties not favored by a high rating have proven to be a more reliable plant than its more highly rated neighbor.

We believe that each variety listed herein is an attractive one, regardless of its rating, and suggest that our customers make their selections from the descriptions only, so that they may judge for themselves the qualities and characteristics of the selection they have made.

Duchesse de Nemours
Each, 75c

Flowerfield Superb PEONY Collection

Four Named Varieties

Karl Rosenfield. Red $0.75
Primevere. White 1.25
Albatre. White-pink .... .60
Mons. Jules Elie. Rose-pink 1.00

$3.60

One of each of these varieties

4 Divisions for $3.00

flowerfield, long island, New York

Sarah Bernhardt — Each 75c

FLOWERFIELD SUPERIOR PEONIES

8.7 **Albatre.** (Crousse.) Late midseason. Large, double type, white with faint pink center and very narrow crimson on edges of a few petals; compact, incurved flower with the tips of outer petals recurved from ball-like center, strong fragrance. Generally considered identical to Avalanche. 60c each.

8.6 **Albert Crousse.** (Grousse.) Late. Large double, light rose-pink having a creamy tone, tinted flesh-pink in a rose-like center when fully opened. Often times called one of the very best late Peonies. Tall and mildly fragrant; a profuse bloomer. 75c each.

7.1 **Alexandre Dumas.** (Guerin.) Early midseason. A pink double with a light violet-rose effect, with a creamy white collar of narrow petals among wide center petals. 75c each.

8.8 **Alsace-Lorraine.** (Lemoine.) Late midseason. A creamy white double of waxy texture with a buff center, rounded petals cupped at the tips, not pointed. Arranged symmetrically in circular form. Unusual in color, a free bloomer of medium size. $1.00 each.

8.0 **Boule de Neige.** (Calot.) Early midseason. A white double with a yellow glow and guards flecked crimson. Outer petals are cupped and surround a fluffy center of narrow petals and stamens. 60c each.

8.6 **Cherry Hill.** (Thurlow.) Very early. Maroon double with a sheen that fairly glistens, carpels are tipped scarlet and together with its yellow stamens appears to brighten the flower. $1.50 each.

8.7 **Claire Dubois.** (Grousse.) Late. Large bright exquisite rose-pink double, very full center, convex and tufted; fringed and incurved petals. One of the very largest Peonies; moderately tall, fragrant, a quite distinct and impressive flower. $1.00 each.

8.1 **Couronne d'Or.** (Calot.) Late. White, full and evenly rounded, double flowers; a ring of yellow stamens appears to illuminate the center. The center petals are crimson tipped. One of the very choicest and most fragrant Peonies. 60c each.

7.7 **Dorchester.** (Richardson.) Early. Pale hydrangea-pink, double, sulphur-white collar without crimson specks. A free bloomer. 60c each.

8.1 **Dr. H. Barnsby.** (Dessert.) Late. A red double Peony of dark old rose tone or light purplish crimson tone. Not too fragrant. Flowers are evenly colored and globular. $1.25 each.

7.8 **Duc de Wellington.** (Calot.) White, guard petals white with sulphur center; an attractive, fragrant flower. $1.00 each.

8.1 **Duchesse de Nemours.** (Calot.) Early. A pure creamy double white with cupped guard petals; a full center of light canary-yellow deepening into a pale green at its base. Its green carpels and stigmas make it a distinctive flower. 75c each.

7.6 **Edulis Superba.** (Lemon.) Early. A very fine bright old rose-pink double, very fragrant. Its strong, tall stems bear large profuse flowers. One of the finest cut flowers, generally considered most deserving of a higher rating. Every garden should have one of these because of its general good qualities. 60c each.

7.8 **E. G. Hill.** (Lemoine.) Another rose-pink double, sometimes called a rich Tyrian rose. A free bloomer with large flowers of a distinct shade. $1.25 each.

8.7 **Elwood Pleas.** (Pleas.) Late. A pink double with flat flowers containing many crinkled petals symmetrically arranged, their pale rose-pink changing to light flesh-pink in the center. Good close set foliage, floriferous. An evenly colored flower about the same shade as Therese. $1.50 each.

8.3 **Eugene Verdier.** (Calot.) Late. A large shell-pink double flower, tinted with cream, compact, usually developing a decided crown; the center appears rose but when fully open has a yellow suffusion from numerous petaloids, sharply defined by their creamy yellow color. It is a floriferous, robust plant with very strong stems. 60c each.

8.4 **Felix Crousse.** (Grousse.) Late midseason. Large brilliant crimson double of even tone and silky luster. Considered by some to be one of the best red Peonies. The blooms are compact, globular and of good form. 75c each.

9.3 **Festiva Maxima.** (Miellez.) Early. A white double that is large, its central petals are flaked crimson; flowers are globular with wide petals of heavy substance and last well when cut. A well-tested old variety, whose popularity has lasted through the years. 60c each.

9.1 **Frances Willard.** (Brand.) Late midseason. A pink-white double. Opens pale pink, changing to white-yellow suffusion in its collar, a hollow symmetrical center develops bearing a few faint red lines; mildly fragrant. Heavy dark foliage, tall with strong stems. $1.00 each.

8.2 **Francois Rousseau.** (Dessert.) Early. Rich crimson, large double type, with a dark silklike sheen becoming lighter toward the base of the petals; a noticeable brightness develops from its buried stamens. Its yellow stamens are disclosed from its rosebud center when fully opened. It is a free bloomer and a vigorous plant. $1.25 each.

8.9 **Georgiana Shaylor.** (Shaylor.) Midseason. A large rose-pink double, paler on the back of petals; a ring of short petals around the center bear vivid crimson marks. It is fragrant but not too strong. Considered by the originator as one of his best specimens. A great exhibition flower. $1.00 each.

8.5 **Germaine Bigot.** (Dessert.) Midseason. A light rose-pink, loosely formed, showing stamens, slowly developing crown and irregularly showing flesh-pink tints and crimson edges. A dependable Peony of medium height with strong stems and good foliage. $1.00 each.

8.2 **Gismonda.** (Grousse.) Very late. Considered generally as one of the handsomest late double pinks; a symmetrical flower with a short creamy collar, dividing the outer petals from the somewhat darker well shaped center. Tall, floriferous, strong stems, and good foliage. 90c each.

7.3 **Golden Harvest.** (Rosenfield.) A pale pink and white double, tinted with salmon and yellow; a free bloomer, and a lovely flower. $1.00 each.

8.4 **Grover Cleveland.** (Terry.) Midseason. A large bright crimson double, mildly fragrant. It is of medium height, fairly floriferous with stiff stems and excellent foliage. A most desirable red with compact large flowers. $1.00 each.

5.7 **Humei.** (Anderson.) A cherry-pink double dwarf plant. Strong foliage, flowers open very quickly and do not keep well when cut. 50c each.

8.7 **James Kelway.** (Kelway.) Early midseason. A pale pink, very large double; the flowers are most attractive, loose and fluffy. Its pale pink color becomes almost white with age but retains a slight flush of pink on its outer petals. 90c each.

8.8 **Karl Rosenfield.** (Rosenfield.) Midseason. A very bright crimson double, containing very little blue. A good clear color with reliable free-flowering blooming habit and exceptionally good form. Its outer petals are large and waved, the central petals are notched and incurved. 75c each.

6.8 **La Coquette.** (Guerin.) A rose color with creamy center, not highly rated but preferred by some over the better rated Peonies because of its attractiveness in the garden. $1.00 each.

Lady Bramwell. A rose-colored Peony considered by many to be Lady Leonora Bramwell. 75c each.

8.3 **La Rosiere.** (Grousse.) Midseason. A semi-double white. It has several rows of long pointed white petals symmetrically arranged like a many-pointed star about a central cluster of yellow stamens. It blooms in huge clusters and is considered one of the loveliest Peonies for the garden. Many feel that this variety should not be disbudded. 75c each.

7.3 **L'Indispensable.** (Unknown.) A lilac-white double whose originator is unknown. 75c each.

8.1 **Livingstone.** (Grousse.) Late. A large double old rose-pink, flaked on a lighter base; a few petals marked crimson, the outer petals occasionally show a light midrib. It has a strong sweet fragrance, strong stems and good foliage, and is free flowering. $1.00 each.

8.4 **Lora Dexheimer.** (Brand.) Midseason. A bright clear and lively crimson double showing a light midrib on the outer petals; the center is incurved, concealing its stamens; it is medium height, floriferous, with strong stems and good foliage. It is one of the best and most popular bright reds. $1.00 each.

flowerfield bulb farm

FLOWERFIELD SUPERIOR PEONIES

Lucie Malard. (Grousse.) A good pink even though not well rated. It bears a large flower and has strong stems. The plant is medium sized with good foliage. 60c each.

8.2 Marcelle Dessert. (Dessert.) Midseason. A very pale pink with minute dots, shading slightly paler in the collar; crimson flecks appear in the center, and when it opens in the late stage, the carpels show greenish yellow, tipped red. Strong stems and foliage. $1.00 each.

8.4 Marguerite Gerard. (Crousse.) Midseason. An immense flesh-pink double, heart-shaped guards and a broad serrated crown of pale flesh-pink, darkening to rose-pink in the center; collar of a few short petals mixed with many yellow stamens. Free flowering, medium height, and good foliage. 60c each.

8.9 Marie Crousse. (Grousse.) Midseason. A pale pink or shaded salmon double, shaded rose in the center. Central petals are broad, narrowing toward the collar, forming an immense globular bloom. A very fine Peony of noteworthy color and form. One of the most beautiful blooms on the show table. $1.50 each.

8.5 Marie Lemoine. (Calot.) Late. Lemon-white with a trace of crimson on the edges of a few petals. Compact and flat at first and develops a large globular form; pure white, with a few yellow petaloids in the collar. Very highly regarded as one of the handsomest Peonies. $1.00 each.

7.8 Marquis C. Lagergren. (Dessert.) A bright crimson double, globular in form, medium height with good foliage. Considered a good red by many, a good garden specimen. $1.25 each.

9.1 Martha Bulloch. (Brand.) Late. A bright old-rose-pink, double. A very remarkable plant and flower, shown in exhibition probably more than any other Peony. It is very tall and bears immense blooms of exquisite beauty and rose-like fragrance. $1.75 each.

8.7 Mary Brand. (Brand.) Midseason. A dark clear crimson double with a brilliant sheen. It carries a few yellow stamens buried in its collar. It has an excellent ball form with overlapping, crinkled and fringed petals. A gorgeous garden decoration. $1.50 each.

7.8 Mlle. Debuisson. (Grousse.) A violet-rose fading to milk-white. A lovely Peony, handsome, with good form and strong foliage. $1.50 each.

8.6 Mme. Auguste Dessert. (Dessert.) Early midseason. Cupped blooms of red-rose-pink, developing a hollow center full of golden yellow stamens and dark rose-pink carpels, flaked crimson on a few petals. A plant of good habits and an excellent garden decoration. A very fine variety. $1.50 each.

8.1 Mme. Calot. (Miellez.) Early. A very light old rose double, shaded somewhat darker toward the crimson-flaked center with a cream collar. A popular cut-flower variety, tall and extremely floriferous. 75c each.

6.8 Mme. Chaumy. (Calot.) A good looking pink double. Its flowers open very quickly, therefore are not lasting. Strong stems and good foliage. 50c each.

6.5 Mme. Coste. (Calot.) The hydrangea-pink guards and sulphur center are most attractive with the collar of cream-white. Occasional crimson flecks on the center stand out well. A good bloomer with strong foliage. 50c each.

7.9 Mme. Crousse. (Calot.) A good white with crimson-flecked center. An attractive garden variety with handsome blooms and strong foliage. 75c each.

7.5 Madame de Galhau. (Grousse.) Late. A good pink double; guards appear almost rosy white around a center of lilac-rose, giving off a good pink appearance. 75c each.

8.2 Mme. D. Treyeran. (Dessert.) Midseason. Large double type. Flesh-pink, thickly overlaid by minute flakes of dark rose-pink blending darker toward the center. A few petals are marked with crimson. Well built, compact flowers with good stems and foliage. $1.00 each.

7.9 Mme. Ducel. (Mechin.) Midseason. A medium size pale old rose double with broad flaring guards and a compact incurved center with a lustrous silvery sheen. Stiff stems, good foliage, and floriferous. Almost identical to Mme. Jules Elie in color and shape, however, it is small and does not feather in center. 75c each.

8.5 Mme. Emile Galle. (Grousse.) Late. Very light rose-pink double defined more strongly in its center, without any crimson markings. A choice variety because of its delicate color, translucent texture and pleasing rose fragrance. Medium height, free flowering with good stems and foliage. 75c each.

8.9 Mme. Emile Lemoine. (Lemoine.) Midseason. A double that opens with outer petals streaked crimson and tiny pink dots appearing like a faint flush. It fades to creamy white with outer petals crimson flaked. $1.00 each.

8.3 Mons. Dupont. (Calot.) Late midseason. A white double with a yellow glow from its buried stamens; central petals are conspicuously blotched with crimson. Very free blooming with tall, stiff stems. 75c each.

9.2 Mons. Jules Elie. (Crousse.) Early. A very large light rose-pink double sort of the opaque quality pink seen in the pink Chrysanthemums. Its guard petals are broad and smooth with center incurved and silvered with light grayish pink. Tall and free flowering, moderately fragrant. $1.00 each.

7.7 Mons. Krelage. (Grousse.) An amaranth-red with silvery tips; a very good garden sort. Medium height good foliage, and free flowering. $1.00 each.

8.8 Mons. Martin Cahuzac. (Dessert.) Early midseason. Large maroon-crimson double, with a black luster. Often said to be the darkest Peony. Medium height, erect, free flowering with stiff stems. $2.00 each.

8.5 Octavie Demay. (Calot.) Early. One of the most popular pale pink doubles. Light old-gold-pink guards with a somewhat darker crown, which develops early with a few splashes of crimson. The distinct collar is composed of narrow, almost white, petals. Considered one of the most attractive and dependable Peonies. 75c each.

Pride of Donay. A red semi-double, dwarf plant; good foliage. Makes a very attractive garden specimen. 50c each.

8.6 Primevere. (Lemoine.) A creamy white anemone type, medium sized, with center composed of short narrow petals of canary-yellow, becoming light with age. Considered one of the best of the so-called yellows. Foliage a good dark green and rather coarse. $1.25 each.

PRIMEVERE
A superior
Peony and
a most attrac-
tive variety.
Each, $1.25.

If you prefer all one
color, or a certain combination of colors, we shall
be glad to fill your order
as you wish it as long as
our stock holds out.

**MONS.
JULES ELIE**
Lovely pink
center, in-
curved silvery
gray.
Each, $1.00.

**SPECIAL
FLOWERFIELD
COLLECTION**

Edulis Superba
Felix Crousse
Festiva Maxima

flowerfield bulb farm — flowerfield,

[20]

ğant Flowers Unequaled for Bouquets

KARL
ROSENFIELD
Each, 75c.

**Flowerfield's
Color Collection**

ONE OF EACH COLOR
White
Pink
Red

3 Divisions of
our Selection **$1.50**

uperba
rousse
Maxima

One each of these
varieties

3 divisions
for **$1.75**)

ALBATRE
A large
double white
with a faint
pink center.
Each, 60c.

werfield, long island, New York

FLOWERFIELD SUPERIOR PEONIES

7.2 **Purpurea Superba.** (Delache.) A deep carmine-rose; guards streaked white, stigmas pink. Flowers are large and well formed, very tall and a free bloomer. $1.25 each.

7.2 **Queen Victoria.** (Kelway.) A good every-day double white. The flower has good substance and color, and in the bud state has a faint blush tint. A good cut-flower variety. $1.00 each.

8.7 **Reine Hortense.** (Calot.) Midseason. Very large rose-pink double, with crisp fluffy petals that are notched and silvered at the tips with an occasional fleck of crimson in the center. Free flowering and tall; considered identical to President Taft. 90c each.

8.8 **Richard Carvel.** (Brand.) Early. A bright crimson large double, with a distinct bluish tinge; broad guard with an irregularly incurved high center. Slightly fragrant, good stems and foliage. $1.25 each.

7.2 **Rubra Superba.** (Richardson.) Late. A magnificent rich brilliant deep crimson without stamens; very large, full and double, and a good cut flower. Foliage good, flower fragrant. $1.50 each.

9.0 **Sarah Bernhardt.** (Lemoine.) Late. One of the strongest growing Peonies, large double type. Dark rose-pink, a trifle lighter at the edges; a few central petals have inconspicuous red edges, and an occasional yellow anther in the collar. Medium height, strong stems, and good foliage. 75c each.

7.9 **Simonne Chevalier.** (Dessert.) A very large pink, compact globular bloom which some would call lilac-rose tinted salmon. The actual effect is pink. Center flecked crimson and tipped silver. 75c each.

9.7 **Solange.** (Lemoine.) Late. A cream-white with a suffusion of buff and pale salmon-pink. A favorite large double of unusual tint about which Peony writers have become enthusiastic. It is considered a greater favorite than Le Cygne. $1.50 each.

7.7 **Suzanne Dessert.** (Dessert & Mechin.) Midseason. Semi-rose type China-pink with silvery tips. Large with very full blooms in clusters. Stands well in full sun. Good foliage and strong stems. $1.25 each.

9.8 **Therese.** (Dessert.) Midseason. An old-rose-pink double with enormous, long, translucent petals, seemingly illuminated by a golden glow in the depths. Heavy foliage, medium height, and strong stems. Truly splendid in texture, color and form. $1.75 each.

7.8 **Triomphe de L'Exposition de Lille.** (Calot.) Large compact blooms of a fresh hydrangea-pink splashed with darker tints of violet-rose with a white reflex. The guard petals change to nearly white. 60c each.

7.4 **Umbellata Rosea.** (Dessert.) Early. A violet-rose with amber-white shadings. A good garden variety, large informal rose type and a free bloomer with good foliage. $1.00 each.

8.3 **Venus.** (Kelway.) Midseason. An old-rose-pink double with a decided lavender tone in the center. Large cupped guards and conical center with a narrow collar of notched petals. A very distinct variety good for garden decoration or cutting. Free blooming, tall with good stems and foliage. $1.00 each.

ℰNorthern Grown Cannas

Cannas have long enjoyed popularity as ornamental plants, prized for their stately habit, strong foliage and showy flowers. For brilliant bedding and massing at modest cost these magnificent summer-blooming flowers cannot be surpassed.

We are proud that our Cannas have long been famous for their sterling quality, immense eyes, and firm substance. The superiority of the hard and firm northern grown Canna is universally recognized although they may be grown commercially with some success in a variety of climatic conditions.

The following varieties have been selected by us after careful tests of hundreds of sorts. Our customers can rely upon them as being the most magnificent and desirable in every respect, combining large flowers of great brilliancy and range of color, with beautiful foliage, free blooming and easy growing qualities.

Strong 2- to 3-eye divisions of any of the following varieties: 15c each; 3 for 40c; $1.50 per doz.

Alsace. Pale sulphur, changing to cream-white. Green foliage. Height 4 feet.

American Red Cross. Glowing scarlet. Green foliage with narrow edge of purple. Height 4 feet.

City of Portland. Deep rich pink. Green foliage. Height 5 feet.

Eureka. The finest white variety; very showy. Green foliage. Height 4 feet.

Halli. One of the most popular pink varieties. Green foliage. Height 3 feet.

King Humbert. Brilliant orange-scarlet with bright red markings. Copper-bronze foliage. Height 4 to 5 feet.

King Midas. Large flowers of a rich pure yellow. Green foliage. Height 4 feet.

Louisiana. Vivid scarlet. Flowers borne in very large trusses. Green foliage. Height 5 feet.

Orange Bedder. Bright orange with some scarlet suffusion. Green foliage. Height 4 to 5 feet.

The Ambassador. Rich cherry-red. Rich bronze foliage and stalk. Height 4 feet.

The President. The outstanding red Canna, having immense trusses of fiery red flowers, produced in great profusion. A vigorous plant, with green foliage. Height 5 feet.

Wintzer's Colossal. Striking, vivid scarlet florets, with green foliage. Height 4 feet.

Wyoming. This is one of the most majestic Cannas in the orchid-flowering class, with the additional attraction of having a luxuriant growth of rich purple foliage. Great plumes of massive orange-colored blossoms. Height 6 feet.

Yellow King Humbert. Orchid-flowering. Flowers are yellow, spotted red. Green foliage. Height 5 feet.

(See Colored Illustrations on Back Cover)

flowerfield bulb farm

Lilies for the Garden

Beautiful in Form and Color

In recent years the hardy varieties of Lilies have gained tremendously in popular favor. With the introductions of the many fascinating and lovely varieties from the Orient, the Lilies are more and more claiming attention as an indispensable part of every garden. As many of the varieties were little known, except to the students of floriculture, it has taken some time for the garden lovers to generally appreciate the range of beauty available in this species, and to further realize that with a relatively limited number of Lilies a continuous show of flowers may be enjoyed from early June until October.

Once established, Lilies increase in beauty each year. They will thrive in any fairly good moist but well-drained garden soil. Most kinds delight in a sunny location but should be mulched to keep the hot sun from the ground around the base of the plants. Lily bulbs differ greatly in size according to kind and variety, and we therefore offer sizes that will give the best results under average conditions.

LILY VARIETIES

Lilium Auratum

An important milestone in floricultural history was marked with the commercial introduction of this Lily in London in the year 1862. This flower, familiarly referred to as "The Golden Rayed Lily" and "The Golden Banded Lily" is still one of the most beautiful and most sought-after members of the family. The flowers, which bloom in August, are white, studded with crimson spots. A gold band passes through the center of each petal. The flowers are large and fragrant, and are carried 15 flowers to a stalk. Must not be planted in soil containing lime. Large bulbs: Each, 35c; 3 for $1.00; $3.50 per doz.

Lilium Batemanniae

One of the most popular garden Lilies. Flowers at about the middle of July. Height about 3 feet. Color clear golden apricot, unspotted. Prefers heavy loam. Each, 25c; 3 for 70c; $2.50 per doz.

Lilium Canadense

A beautiful and vigorous woodland variety which does fairly well in the open. It thrives best in moist and leaf-mold soils. Two forms of Canadense exist; both having bright orange, brown-speckled hues predominating:

Canadense Flavum. Height 3 to 5 feet. Bell-shaped golden flowers. Each, 20c; 3 for 55c; $2.00 per doz.

Canadense Rubrum. A selected red form of the above. Each, 25c; 3 for 70c; $2.50 per doz.

Lilium Concolor

A relatively old member of the Lily family, originally introduced from China in 1806. The flowers, as the name implies, are of uniform bright scarlet. They average 3 inches across, are carried four to a stalk, and bloom during late June and early July. A very dependable variety which thrives in the colder parts of the United States, and is especially splendid for the rock garden. Each, 25c; 3 for 70c; $2.50 per doz.

Lilium Dauricum (Candlestick Lily)

A fine, easily grown, garden Lily introduced from Siberia in 1745. The flowers are orange-red, spotted with purplish black, and are carried upright three to six on a stalk. Blooms during the later part of July, attaining a height of 2 to 3 feet. Each, 25c; 3 for 70c; $2.50 per doz.

Lilium Elegans (Thunbergianum)

An early-blooming dwarf Lily of the easiest possible garden culture. It is especially suitable for mass effects for the large, upright, cup-shaped flowers very striking in appearance. We have selected, and present here, the best forms of Lilium Elegans.

Alice Wilson. Lovely lemon-yellow spotted flowers. Height 2 feet. Each, 35c; 3 for $1.00; $3.50 per doz.

Atrosanguineum. Deep rich crimson with purple spots at base of petals. Height 1 foot. Each, 35c; 3 for $1.00; $3.50 per doz.

Hirtellus. A beautiful deep shade of orange, almost clear except for slight speckling. Height about 18 inches. Each, 40c; 3 for $1.10; $4.00 per doz.

Incomparable. Rich orange with black spots. Quite similar but an improvement over Lilium Elegans, Leonard Joerg. Height 12 inches. Each, 40c; 3 for $1.10; $4.00 per doz.

Kimbusen. A deep red-orange-centered flower with spotted petals. Grows about 12 to 18 inches tall. Each, 40c; 3 for $1.10; $4.00 per doz.

Lilium Hansoni

No other Lily is so completely dependable in its growing habits, so sure to thrive and bloom, and possesses so many virtues. Among these is its apparent immunity from all forms of disease and insect pests. It usually grows about 2 or 3 feet high, although a height of six or more feet is not uncommon. The flowers bloom in midsummer, are a striking clear golden yellow with red-brown spots, and are carried six to fifteen on a stalk. They possess fine substance and are delightfully fragrant. For outdoor planting a soil rich in humus is preferable. Indoors they are admirable planted three to a pot. Each, 40c; 3 for $1.10; $4.00 per doz.

Lilies for

Lilium Henryi

Known also as "Orange Speciosum," this late-blooming garden Lily has rated exceedingly high ever since its introduction in 1888. Because 25 to 30 beautiful rich orange flowers are often carried on a single 7-ft. stalk, it is advisable to stake the plants. This Lily is perfectly hardy and will thrive in any soil but should be planted rather deeply, 8 inches to 1 foot, in well-drained ground, and preferably in a partly shaded spot. Each, 35c; 3 for $1.00; $3.50 per doz.

Lilium Leichtlini

A rather scarce Lily having orange to dull red reflexed flowers with brownish spots. The stalks carry about 6 to 10 flowers and seldom rise more than 24 inches, growing as they do from a comparatively small bulb. Each, 50c; 3 for $1.40; $5.00 per doz.

Lilium Philadelphicum

A small but daintily attractive woodland species. The bulbs are small and send up stems 1 to 3 feet high, carrying about 3 bright orange cup-shaped flowers. The petal tips are colored darker and are spotted with maroon. This Lily is fine for naturalizing and for use in shady nooks, and is perfectly hardy. Each, 25c; 3 for 70c; $2.50 per doz.

Lilium Regale (Myriophyllum)

A wonderful garden Lily of amazing hardiness which thrives and propagates under the most severe conditions. Strong, vigorous stems, rising about 4 feet, carry 6 or more graceful trumpet-shaped fragrant flowers whose coloring is a pink suffused white with a yellow center, blending upwards on the trumpet. Each, 25c; 3 for 70c; $2.50 per doz.

Lilium Speciosum

One of the most popular Lilies because of its showiness and reliability. One of the latest bloomers, it provides color in the garden during the later part of October and even early November. Three of the best forms of Speciosum are offered:

Lilium Speciosum Album. Beautiful pure white flowers with green lines on each petal. Delightfully and strongly fragrant. Very hardy. Each, 40c; 3 for $1.10; $4.00 per doz.

Lilium Speciosum, Melpomene. The outstanding form of the species, possessing the richest shades of crimson with deep spots and contrasting silvery white edging. Very vigorous and hardy. Each, 45c; 3 for $1.25; $4.50 per doz.

Lilium Speciosum Rubrum. In form this flower characterizes the Speciosum types. Its blooms are rose-colored, with a pleasant softness which contrasts with the more brilliant forms above. Each, 35c; 3 for $1.00; $3.50 per doz.

Lilium Henryi. 35c each; 3 for $1.00.

←
Lilium Speciosum Rubrum
The petals are well rolled back and handsomely spotted with rose-red over light rose background with white-suffused edges. Price: 35c each; 3 for $1.00.

➡
Lilium Davuricum
(The Candlestick Lily)
Blooms in late July; flowers orange-red, spotted with purplish black. Blossoms 5 in. across. Price: 25c each; 3 for 70c.

flowerfield bulb farm

[24]

the Garden

Lilium Superbum

A showy variety whose striking appearance has won for itself the picturesque name of the "American Turk's-Cap Lily." Stately and at the same time graceful, it possesses great vigor and grows as high as 9 feet and sometimes carries 50 flowers on a stalk. The flowers themselves are bright orange-red, shading towards yellow and spotted with violet-brown. It is native to swampy lands but thrives well in drier ground, being particularly adaptable to Rhododendron beds and garden borders. Each, 30c; 3 for 85c; $3.00 per doz.

Lilium Tigrinum

The familiar Tiger Lily with brilliant orange-salmon flowers having purple spots on the inner surfaces. Several forms exist from which we have chosen two of the most interesting and reliable:

Lilium Tigrinum Splendens. A late bloomer with large flowers and leaves and generally vigorous characteristics. It grows as much as 7 feet high. Each, 25c; 3 for 70c; $2.50 per doz.

Lilium Tigrinum Flore-Pleno. The Double Tiger Lily which is gaining so much interest among garden enthusiasts. It blooms late in the season, grows about 3 feet high and its double flowers are very lovely and make it a really fine and worth-while Lily, especially for mass color effects. Each, 30c; 3 for 85c; $3.00 per doz.

Lilium Umbellatum

An easily grown early-flowering Lily which blooms in June. It is well suited to both naturalizing and garden border use. Each, 30c; 3 for 85c; $3.00 per doz.

Lilium Speciosum Album
Price: 40c each; 3 for $1.10.

Lilium Tigrinum Splendens
The popular Tiger Lily, with brilliant orange-salmon flowers and purple spots. Price: 25c each; 3 for 70c.

Lilium Alice Wilson
A very dwarf variety of a lemon-yellow color, shading darker in the center. Price: 35c each; 3 for $1.00.

flowerfield, long island, New York

Exhibition Dahlias

Present a Great Variety in Form and Color

One of the most popular garden plants we have today. It is of easy culture, has a wealth of beautiful colors, in addition to having diverse forms such as cactus, semi-cactus, formal decorative, informal decorative, in the large flowering type; the pompon and the miniatures in the small flowering type.

A well-known author on garden subjects wrote about the Dahlia as follows:

"The Dahlia is the busy man's flower—robust, reliable, repaying a small amount of care with a wealth of bloom at a season when the rest of the garden too often is at tag-ends.

"A flower, too, for one who likes to build up a stock of his or her raising, for the increase each year is fourfold or more. No sunny spot of ground that is reasonably well drained, need be without its Dahlias, for they are immensely adaptable. Any lack of soil fertility can be made up by artificial means."

Adirondack Sunset. I. D. A brilliant scarlet with golden tips, center tipped with golden orange, with reverse side of petals flushed with gold. Blooms are large and carried on good stems. Each, 75c; 3 for $2.00.

Amelia Earhart. S. C. A pleasing shade of apricot-buff with salmon tints, shades to soft yellow at the base. Large blooms. Each, $1.50; 3 for $4.25.

America's Sweetheart. F. D. Large pure yellow blooms carried erect on long stems. Each, $1.50; 3 for $4.25.

Ann Benedict. F. D. Splendid dark red on stems that are always erect. Plants of good foliage. Each, $1.50; 3 for $4.25.

Arelda Lloyd. I. D. A good lemon-yellow on strong stems. Blooms large and deep with the good qualities of Jane Cowl, which it resembles except in color. Each, $1.50; 3 for $4.25.

Avalon. F. D. A well-formed rich lemon-yellow Dahlia. Each, 50c; 3 for $1.25.

Barbara Redfern. I. D. A vigorous plant bearing large blossoms of old rose and old gold beautifully blended. Flowers are borne on strong stems. Each, 50c; 3 for $1.25.

Beauty Supreme. F. D. Similar to Jersey's Beauty in form and an excellent cut flower. Color, a pleasing orchid shade. Each, 60c; 3 for $1.50.

Buckeye King. F. D. A rich glowing gold color. Each, 75c; 3 for $2.00.

California Idol. I. D. An immense flower of glistening yellow. Blooms are very deep and carried on stout stems. One of the largest Dahlias. Each, $1.00; 3 for $2.75.

California Rose. I. D. Large graceful flowers of bright rose. Is an excellent cut flower. Each, $1.50; 3 for $4.25.

Cavalcade. F. D. Large blooms, mulberry and old rose, carried on good stems. Perfect form. Each, $1.50; 3 for $4.25.

Champoeg. I. D. Strikingly immense blooms of waxy yellow shading to a salmon-red at the outer edges of the petals. Backs of petals are yellow. Each, 50c; 3 for $1.25.

Cigarette. A creamy white heavily edged with reddish orange. A very good but different cut flower. Each, 50c; 3 for $1.25.

Clara Carder. I. D. A giant clear cyclamen-pink. Each, $1.00; 3 for $2.75.

Dr. J. H. Carman. F. D. Rose colored tipped with silver. An excellent cut flower. Each, 50c; 3 for $1.25.

Eagle Rock Fantasy. Large, deep blooms of clear mallow-pink. Stout stems. Each, 75c; 3 for $2.00.

Edith Gille. F. D. A bluish lavender Jersey's Beauty. A selected strain of Beauty Supreme. Each, 75c; 3 for $2.00.

Elite Glory. F. D. Bright red, on stout stems. One of the largest Dahlias. Each, 50c; 3 for $1.25.

Elkridge. I. D. Pure white on long straight stems. One of the best whites. Each, 35c; 3 for 90c.

Ella May. C. A free blooming cactus Dahlia of crimson-carmine. Flowers are medium large and have full centers. Each, 50c; 3 for $1.25.

El Toreador. F. D. Brilliant red on long straight stems. Excellent cut flower. Each, 25c; 3 for 60c.

Forest Fire. I. D. Big flashy blooms of bright scarlet-flame and splashes of yellow. Each, $1.50; 3 for $4.25.

Francis Larocco. F. D. Large yellow and long stems. One of the best cut flowers. Each, 25c; 3 for 60c.

F. T. D. F. D. Beautiful pink flowers carried on long strong stems. Flowers are very well shaped. Each, 75c; 3 for $2.00.

Franklin D. Roosevelt. F. D. Fine deep flowers of bright carmine-red. Each, 75c; 3 for $2.00.

Gallant Fox. F. D. An outstanding Dahlia of luminous dark red. Six-inch flowers. Each, 35c; 3 for 90c.

Golden Beauty. I. D. Pinkish yellow. More accurately described as apricot-yellow splashed with jasper-pink. Each, $1.50; 3 for $4.25.

Golden Eclipse. F. D. Large deep perfect blooms of golden yellow with a blush of salmon. Each, 60c; 3 for $1.50.

Golden Goblin. F. D. Large blooms of rich gold. Stems are long and strong. Each, 50c; 3 for $1.25.

Gold Standard. C. Golden tan, darker toward the center. Large blooms carried on long slender stems. Each, $1.25; 3 for $3.50.

Hunt's Velvet Wonder. I. D. Big deep flowers on extra strong stems. Color, a rich bright violet-burgundy. Under some lights it appears royal purple. Each, $1.25; 3 for $3.50.

James Kirby. I. D. A beautiful crimson-scarlet with ruby tones at the center. One of the best reds. Flowers held erect on stems 3 feet long. Each, 75c; 3 for $2.00.

Jane Cowl. I. D. One of the best known Dahlias. A rich bronze-buff and gold. Each, 35c; 3 for 90c.

Jean Kerr. F. D. A perfectly shaped white Dahlia which has all the good qualities of strong, straight stems. An early and free bloomer. A good cut flower. Each, 35c; 3 for 90c.

Jersey's Beacon. F. D. (See color illustration on page 29.) A large well-formed flower. Chinese red with a paler reverse, making a very lovely two-toned effect. Each, 35c; 3 for 90c.

DAHLIA RAINBOW MIXTURE

Select Your Own Color

Six Tubers for		Twelve Tubers for	
$1.50		**$2.50**	
Red	Copper	Orchid	Yellow
White	Pink	Purple	Apricot

flowerfield bulb farm

EXHIBITION DAHLIAS

Jersey's Beauty. F. D. (See page 28 for colored illustration.) The most popular and best known Dahlia. Considered unsurpassed for exhibition or garden blooms. Flowers are a lovely shade of rose-pink, and perfectly formed. This Dahlia possesses all the good qualities of growth, stem form and keeping as a cut flower. Each, 25c; three for 60c.

Jersey's Triumph. F. D. Bright copper, flushed salmon-bronze. Each, 30c; 3 for 75c.

Jim Moore. I. D. Primrose-yellow, suffused with salmon-pink. A vigorous grower. Each, 50c; 3 for $1.25.

Kentucky. F. D. (Color illustration on page 28.) A sport of Jersey's Beauty, having all its favorable qualities, but distinctly different in color. A bronze-pink, resulting from pink blended with gold. Each, 25c; 3 for 60c.

Kentucky Red. I. D. An attractive flaming scarlet. Does not fade. Each, 50c; three for $1.25.

King Midas. I. D. An enormous clear yellow, high full center. Free bloomer and grower. Each, 35c; three for 90c.

Kiss Me. S. C. A very popular and unusual flower. An attractive and distinct bicolor of red and white. Blooms freely, and is a very fine cut flower. Each, 40c; three for $1.00.

Lord of Autumn. I. D. A rich clear yellow. Blooms are immense and very deep. One of the most beautiful Dahlias. Each, $1.00; three for $2.75.

Margaret Mason. F. D. Showy flowers of silver-rose-pink. Each, 75c; three for $2.00.

Margaret Woodrow Wilson. I. D. A large creamy white flower suffused with pink. Could also be described as an opalescent pink. Each, 30c; 3 for 75c.

Marshall's Beauty. F. D. Lovely rose-pink with delicate shadings of lavender-lilac. Each, 40c; 3 for $1.00.

Marshall's Pink. F. D. (See color illustration on page 29.) A fine pink. A vigorous grower; stems are long and strong. A very fine cut flower. Each, 50c; three for $1.25.

Mrs. George Le Boutellier. I. D. A fine bright velvety red. Grows to immense size without extra care. Stems are stout and strong, and plants sturdy and healthy. Each, $1.25; three for $3.50.

Myra Howard. I. D. Color pure gold with a rose sheen. Another huge flower that glistens in the sunlight to improve any garden. Each, 75c; three for $2.00.

Omar. Khayyam. F. D. Very large flowers, strong stems. Chinese red, shading to orange and then even lighter at the tips of the petals. An unusual coloring. Each, 75c; 3 for $2.00.

Red Wonder. I. D. Rich cerise-red, as the flower opens the center is amber, changing to amber shaded petal tips. Each, 50c; 3 for $1.25.

Robert E. Lee. S. C. Brilliant cardinal-red that does not fade in bright sunlight. A very nice cut flower, strong stems. Each, 50c; three for $1.25.

Sagamore Gold. F. D. A pure golden yellow. Flowers are large and beautifully formed. Each, 25c; three for 60c.

Spotlight. I. D. Huge sulphur-yellow, light at tips. Each, 60c; three for $1.50.

Star of Bethlehem. S. C. (See color illustration on page 28.) A white cactus Dahlia. Perfectly shaped and pure white, making a distinctive appearance. Flowers are held above the rich green foliage. Each, 75c; three for $2.00.

Sultan of Hillcrest. I. D. Clear deep lemon-yellow. Reverse of petals rosy pink. Petals recurve to stem to give an unusual color effect. Blooms are very large. Each, $1.00; three for $2.75.

Thomas Edison. F. D. Royal purple best describes the color of this Dahlia. Flowers are beautifully shaped and large, on sturdy stems. Each, 50c; three for $1.25.

White King. F. D. Perfectly shaped white that is an excellent cut flower. Each, 30c; three for 75c.

White Wonder. I. D. Large fluffy white. Long graceful petals. Each, 40c; three for $1.00.

Miniature Dahlias

Excellent for Decorative Purposes

Miniature Dahlias are exact replicas of the large flowered types. The flowers are perfectly shaped and exquisitely colored. In size the miniatures are between the pompons and the exhibition types. Much of their popularity is due to their excellence as a cut flower.

We offer the following at 50c each; $5.00 per doz.; or 2 tubers of each of the following varieties for $5.00.

Baby Beauty. F. D. A miniature Jersey's Beauty.

Baby Royal. S. C. Salmon shading to apricot.

Coronne. I. D. Pure white.

Eclipse, Jr. F. D. Deep gold.

Fairy. F. D. Rose-pink with lavender tints.

Market Queen. I. D. Red and white.

flowerfield, long island, New York

Exhibition Dahlias - *Every One a Winner*

5 EXHIBITION DAHLIA COLLECTION

This collection includes one each of the five
varieties shown on pages 28 and 29

1 Jersey's Beauty   1 Jersey's Beacon
1 Kentucky   1 Marshall's Pink
1 Star of Bethlehem

All 5 for $2.00

15 (3 each of 5 kinds) $5.75

JERSEY'S BEAUTY
The most popular and best known
Dahlia; an ideal pink for exhibition.
Each, 25c; 3 for 60c.

KENTUCKY
An unusual color tone of pink over
a yellow-brown, resembling old gold;
excellent for cutting. Each, 25c; 3
for 60c.

STAR OF BETHLEHEM
A pure white Cactus Dahlia with a
high full center resembling a star.
Each, 75c; 3 for $2.00.

flowerfield bulb farm

[28]

POMPON DAHLIAS

Any of the following varieties, 25c each.

AMBER QUEEN. Button-like blooms of amber shaded to apricot. Flowers are borne on wiry stems well above the dark foliage.

BRONZE BEAUTY. A beautiful autumn shade, golden bronze.

EDGAR. A small perfect bloom of cream-tinted yellow.

EDITH MULLER. Beautiful rose-red, blended with rich creamy yellow.

GANYMEDE. Small blooms of fawn-pink.

GIRLIE. Lovely little flower of lilac-mauve.

GOLDEN QUEEN. Splendid blooms, rich yellow. A good cut flower.

HAZEL. An unusual shade of buff shading to brown. A profuse bloomer.

HESPERIA. Small, compact yellow blooms.

HONEY. Yellow flowers faintly suffused with light red toward the ends of the petals.

INDIAN CHIEF. A perfectly shaped flower of bright red tipped with white. An unusual cut flower, a good keeper and a free bloomer.

JOE FETTE. Pure white blooms. Reliable for lots of blooms each season and as a cut flower.

KLEINE DOMITEA. An odd flower of delicate buff with a lavender center.

LADY MARY HOPE. Red and white.

LITTLE DAVID. A russet orange pom, perfectly formed. A good cut flower and profuse bloomer.

LITTLE DEAR. A beautifully colored flower. Old rose with salmon shadings.

LITTLE DOROTHEA. One of the most popular pompons. Bright orange with white markings.

LITTLE HERMAN. A deep red flower with white-tipped petals. Very symmetrical.

LITTLE MARY. A good free bloomer. Long-stemmed. Color light maroon.

MARY MUNNS. Long stems, fuchsia-red flowers. Blooms profusely.

PRINCE CHARMING. Velvety maroon. Long stems.

ROSE WILMOTH. A rose-pink. Flowers are small and graceful.

SUNNY DAYBREAK. A well formed Pompon Dahlia of bright apricot, edged with red.

Any three of the above for 60c; $2.25 per doz.

JERSEY'S BEACON
A lovely Chinese red with a buff reflex, giving a two-tone effect, making a most attractive formal decorative variety. Each, 35c; 3 for 90c.

flowerfield, long island, New York

MARSHALL'S PINK
A very strong grower with long, stiff stems. Each, 50c; 3 for $1.25.

4 Summer Flowering Novelties

HYACINTHUS CANDICANS

Galtonia, Giant Summer Hyacinth or Cape Hyacinth

A handsome species of Hyacinth which blossoms during the summer and early fall, growing 3 to 5 feet high, with spikes 2 feet in length, of 20 to 30 thimble-shaped white flowers. Planted in the spring, they bloom in August, September, and even October, a bed of a dozen or more bulbs producing a grand effect. The bulbs are hardy in localities having moderate winters, and do best in a rich and moist soil.

Strong bulbs, each 20c; 3 for 55c; $2.00 per doz.

CHLIDANTHUS FRAGRANS

Tropical American summer-flowering bulbs; allied to zephyranthes. This bulb is a revelation of beauty. It is much like an amaryllis with a strong bulb which starts growth as soon as potted and is soon in bloom. The golden yellow flowers are pleasantly fragrant and are borne in clusters of 4 to 6 on a stalk.

Two or three spikes of these exquisite large yellow blossoms are produced at each blooming period. Pot the bulbs at any time, winter or spring, or plant outdoors in spring. Strong bulbs, each, 15c; three for 40c; $1.50 per doz.

Hyacinthus Candicans

MADEIRA VINE (Boussingaultia) or CLIMBING MIGNONETTE

This lovely vine is much prized for adorning porches and arbors. Ten to twenty feet of vine grow from the tuberous roots in a season. The foliage is most attractive and remains free from insects throughout the summer. An abundance of delightfully fragrant white flowers bloom in late summer and fall.

The plant will not withstand frost but is hardy if given protection in localities having mild winters.

Extra-large, selected tubers, 4 to 6 inches long; 20c each; 3 for 50c; $2.00 per doz.
Large, No. 1 tubers, 3 to 4 inches long; 15c each; 3 for 40c; $1.50 per doz.
Medium, No. 2 tubers, 2 to 3 inches long; 10c each; 3 for 25c; $1.00 per doz.

Madeira Vine

ISMENE CALATHINA GRANDIFLORA

Peruvian Daffodil or Basket Flower

A stately and impressive summer-flowering bulb having very large snowy white Amaryllis-like blooms which are delightfully fragrant. It is really one of the most lovely of all the Amaryllis tribe, and is very easy to grow. Our bulbs are large and strong and begin to flower in two or three weeks after planting, sending up tall flower stems which bear several of its magnificent blossoms.

As a pot plant it is excellent, and as a garden bulb, treated like a Gladiolus, it is one of the choicest of all flowers.

The bulbs should be kept in a dry and warm place until June, at which time they should be planted in a well-drained fertile soil. They will multiply plentifully, and in October should be taken up and stored away.

Strong bulbs, each 25c; 3 for 65c; per doz., $2.50.

Ismene Calathina

flowerfield bulb farm

Superior Plant Food and Fertilizers

The New Improved Fertilizer and Lawn Seed Distributor

This easy running, sturdy, and well-built Seed and Fertilizer Distributor gives you an even and economical distribution. It saves your time and insures better results. Easily adjusted to any of our Lawn Seed Mixtures or Fertilizers. Full instructions for its use as imprinted on the back of the Distributor.

Prices $6.50 to $22.75

4 SIZES
Home Lawn Distributor. 25 pounds capacity, $6.50.
M 180. 18 in wide, 40-50 pounds capacity. $11.00.
M 241. 24 in. wide, 65-75 pounds capacity. $16.00.
M 361. 36 in. wide, 100-120 pounds capacity. $22.75

Gorgeous Flowers

— HEALTHIER, MORE COLORFUL

Now—the balanced plant food professional growers use . . . available for the home gardener. AGRICO FOR GARDENS — stimulates deeper root growth, stiffer stalks, more and finer blooms. With just the right blend of ALL the plant food elements your garden needs. Clean, odorless, safe, easy to use. Try some—now.

FOR BETTER GARDENS
Made especially for
FLOWERS & VEGETABLES

AGRICO

A COMPLETE PLANT FOOD

MANUFACTURED ONLY BY
The AMERICAN AGRICULTURAL CHEMICAL Co
NEW YORK

Fertilize Your Garden, Lawn, Shrubs and Trees

YOU SAVE MONEY BY USING GOOD FERTILIZER

GREENER LAWNS
HEALTHIER
TREES AND SHRUBS

Have a lawn everybody admires . . . rich, luxuriant growth of grass that stays green all summer. Use this truly complete fertilizer, specially blended with ALL the plant foods needed to produce a beautiful lawn. Use Agrico on trees and shrubs, too. Clean, odorless, safe, easy to use.

AGRICO   THE NATION'S LEADING FERTILIZER

Have you ever wondered why your flowers weren't as fine as the pictures in the catalog? Or why your vegetable garden fell short of expectations? If so, just try **Agrico** for gardens, the truly complete plant food that is especially formulated to do this one job and do it better than any all-purpose fertilizer can possibly do.

Agrico gives you the kind of results professional growers get. It's the fertilizer used the country over by leading florists and greenhousemen...the fertilizer the most successful farmers use — men who plant 50, 100, even 500 acres of corn, potatoes, and other crops.

In flowers, Agrico brings out the full beauty and rich coloring inherent in good seed and choice quality bulbs. In vegetables, Agrico develops succulent, full-flavored produce, rich in health-giving mineral nutrients. Remember, there are two grades of Agrico for the home garden — AGRICO FOR GARDENS and AGRICO FOR LAWNS, TREES, and SHRUBS. Use Agrico on your lawn and in your garden this year, and see the difference it makes.

We are only offering Fertilizer manufactured by the American Agricultural Chemical Company because we feel that their long experience and fine reputation in the field of commercial Fertilizers recommends their product as one of the best produced today.

AGRICO for Lawns, Trees, and Shrubs		AGRICO for Garden	
5 lbs.	$0.45	5 lbs.	$0.45
10 lbs.	.75	10 lbs.	.75
25 lbs.	1.50	25 lbs.	1.40
50 lbs.	2.50	50 lbs.	2.40
100 lbs.	4.00	100 lbs.	3.75

Ask for our special quantity prices on 500 lbs or more for shipment at one time.

Flowerfield, long island, New York

ANEMONE

Hardy and attractive flower garden and border plants of French origin. They have been popular for their beautiful show of flowers, which are admirable for cutting, and are prized by many for their striking foliage.

They thrive best in a fresh, rather rich, sandy loam, well-drained; but most of the species will do well in any good garden soil. Early spring planting is best in the northern states, while fall planting is preferable in southern climes.

St. Brigid. Double and semi-double flowers in a variety of colors: White, Lavender, Blue, Violet, Pink, and Crimson. Any color, each 15c; 3 for 40c; $1.40 per doz.

St. Brigid strain in mixed colors. 3 for 25c; 75c per doz.

His Excellency. Exceptional as a cut flower. Brilliant poppy-scarlet petals with a center almost pure black. Each, 10c; 3 for 25c; 90c per doz.

St. Brigid

Outstanding Seed Novelties for 1939

4524 Morning Glory, Scarlett O'Hara
Gold Medal 1939 A. A. S.

The sensational introduction for this year. Scarlett O'Hara is an entirely new color break in this popular garden flower, a rich dark wine-red or deep rosy crimson. The flowers measure about 4 inches in diameter and are freely produced on fast growing vines which start blooming within 65 days after the seed is sown. The dark green foliage does not make a heavy growth, giving the plants a very graceful appearance, especially when covering arbors and trellises. Pkt., 25c; 3 for 65c.

2338 Scabiosa, Imperial Giants, Blue Moon

Hybridists in their unending quest for new flowers are ofttimes astounded by the unsuspected beauty they have succeeded in producing by their plant guidance and care. This glorious achievement was accomplished by the very excellent hybridizing technique practiced by Bodger, who has introduced this magnificent flower. Instead of flowers composed of a few rows of broad petals surmounted by a flat pincushion-like top of small petals, this new introduction has flowers composed entirely of broad, heavy, waxy petals, eliminating the pincushion center entirely. In other words, the flower is literally fully double. They are extremely large, 2¾ inches across and 2 to 2¾ inches deep, about the shape of an old-fashioned beehive.

The color is a rich deep lavender-blue, a shade which maintains the effectiveness indoors and out. The plant is upright, 42 to 48 inches in height, its stems are strong and wiry and hold the flowers proudly erect. It is ideal for cutting because of its long, 27-inch stems. Pkt., 25c; 3 for 65c.

4524— Scarlett O'Hara Pkt., 25c

5001 Marigold, Sunrise

A marvelous new strain of Marigold discovered in Canada by Mr. W. H. Gale and subsequently developed by the company he represents. The flowers are large and ball-shaped, composed of dozens of tiny five-petaled florets, gracefully interlocking and daintily fringed in effect. The color is brilliant golden yellow, a dazzling pure beauty. They are 100 per cent fully double and commence to bloom around August 15th. Pkt., 25c; 3 for 65c.

5002 Petunia, Ruffled Giant, Marilyn

This ruffled Giant type of Petunia has much greater individual beauty than many other varieties and because the popularity of salmon colored garden flowers is unquestioned, Petunia Marilyn should be one of the leading selections for this season. Ruffled flowers, but not fringed, 4 to 5 inches diameter, in a glowing shade of salmon-rose strongly veined a deeper salmon-rose. The overall salmon color blends delicately lighter toward its ruffled edges. Unquestionably one of the most attractively colored of any Petunia. Pkt., 35c; 3 for 90c.

5003 Zinnia Fantasy, White Light
Recommended 1938 A. A. S.

Again Hybridizer Bodger triumphed with their Fantasy Zinnias and received for the third time, recognition in the All-America Selections with their new introduction White Light, which is considered a very worthy successor to Star Dust and The Mixture, both of which were granted Awards of Merit at the time of their introduction.

The color is nearest to white as any Zinnia yet developed. It is medium sized, shaggy petaled, a pure restful little beauty, lovely in vases or in the garden. It lends a soft note of restfulness to any location selected for it. Pkt., 25c; 3 for 65c.

2338—Scabiosa, Blue Moon. Pkt., 25c

[32]

flowerfield bulb farm

$\mathcal{F}$ine $\mathcal{A}$nnual $\mathcal{F}$lower Seeds

GENERAL LIST OF ANNUAL FLOWERS

Annual flowers live a short but resplendent life. The seeds germinate, produce the mature plants, flower, and die all within the first summer season. They are sown where they are to flower, and do not require starting in artificial heat with its subsequent transplanting outdoors.

Most annuals prefer a sunny and open position in deeply cultivated soil. It is important that the earth be thoroughly forked, broken up, and then raked finely in order that the tiny, hair-like rootlets can get a good start in their growth.

Plant annual flower seeds on a clear, dry day if possible, and distribute the seed very thinly. The seed can be sown in shallow grooves made with a hoe or a piece of wood, or they can be scattered broadcast over the area, and then covered lightly with fine soil.

AGERATUM (Floss Flower)

1000 Blue Perfection. One of the finest and deepest hued specimens in this popular family of summer-flowering annuals. The large fluffy blooms form dense clusters of an exquisitely deep amethyst-blue during late summer and early fall. Height 9 inches. Pkt., 10c; 3 pkts., 25c.

ALYSSUM (Madwort)

4035 Carpet of Snow. A well-named annual which grows so profusely that it gives the effect of a white carpet upon the ground. It is one of the very best plants for beds, rock gardens, and for edgings as it grows about 4 inches high and spreads rapidly and evenly, forming a lovely mass of white blossoms from spring to late autumn. Pkt., 10c; 3 pkts., 25c.

AMARANTHUS
(Joseph's Coat)

4041 Tricolor Splendens. Relatively tall annuals which grow about 3 ft. high. The foliage is brilliantly variegated in rich glowing scarlet, yellow, and green. The plant is well suited to background arrangements or for occasional groupings. The plant thrives in a hot, sunny location, and does best in a soil which is rich in lime. Pkt., 10c; 3 pkts., 25c.

ANCHUSA
(Summer Forget-Me-Not)

4045 Blue Bird. This is undoubtedly one of the finest blue annuals for beds and borders. The dwarf compact plants, 15 in. high, carry beautiful indigo-blue flowers which bloom from early summer until late fall. Pkt., 10c; 3 pkts., 25c.

ANTIRRHINUM
(Snapdragon)

SUPER MAJESTIC RUST - PROOF STRAIN. These new and modern giants grow 2 to 2½ ft. high with 10 to 20 brilliantly colorful spikes blooming at the same time. The flowers of this fine strain are individually large and unusually broad. Thanks to the hybridizer's skill, the foliage resists the rust disease. This flower is very desirable for beds and borders and cuts well.
4724 New Red Shades.
4725 New Pink Shades.
4727 Mixed. Balanced blend of all the newest shades and named varieties. Any of the above: 15c per pkt; 3 pkts., 35c.

ARCTOTIS

NEW HYBRIDS, AUTUMN SHADES
4053 Among the dozens of colorful winter and spring blooming flowers none is more gay and cheerful than these New Autumn Shades in the popular Arctotis Hybrids. The plants are attractively compact and fairly long-stemmed with the flowers above the foliage. The colors include many beautiful tones of red, orange, burnt orange, bronzy orange, and many shades of yellow and cream; all tipped autumn tones. The foliage is soft gray-green with slender wavy-edged leaves. These hybrids are an outstanding addition to the border garden. Pkt., 25c; 3 pkts., 65c.

ASTERS

No garden is complete without Asters. These easily grown annuals bloom perfectly within 3 to 4 months after planting in any good, well-drained soil where they may have plenty of sunshine and moisture.

AMERICAN BRANCHING, WILT-RESISTANT. Fine robust plants 2½ to 3 ft. tall, with firm branching stems. The flowers are large, double, and of perfect form, blooming in early September. All of the varieties listed below are selected stocks, and are the very best available, regardless of cost.

1064 Beauty Crimson. An improved strain in this color. Pkt., 10c.

1065 Peerless Pink. Delicate shell-pink. Pkt., 10c.

1066 Azure-Blue. A beautiful tone of azure to dark lavender. Pkt., 10c.

4067 Mixed. A fine mixture of the named varieties and many others; all wilt-resistant. Pkt., 10c.

> **AMERICAN BRANCHING ASTER COLLECTION**
> One packet of each of the above 3 varieties, and one packet of mixed—
> Four Packets for only 30c.

IMPROVED CREGO WILT-RESISTANT. Robust branching plants about 2½ ft. tall. The flowers are large, double, well shaped, and bloom in mid-September. The color range is extremely wide and includes blues: azure, navy, dark and light, also crimson, orchid, deep rose, salmon, peach, shell-pink, and white.

4727—Rust-Proof Antirrhinum. Pkt., 15c

ASTERS—Continued
2157 Peach-Blossom.
2193 Shell-Pink.
2195 White.
2075 Mixed. Finest blend of the above colors and many others.
Price of above Asters: 10c per pkt.; 3 for 25c.

SUPER GIANT

4066 El Monte. This is the largest and most satisfactory double Aster class known. The flowers measure from 6 to 8 in. across, with full-petaled, graceful, interlacing petals. This fine florist's variety won the Silver Medal Award in the 1936 All-America Selections. The blooms come out early and are a striking, glowing crimson. The plants grow 2½ ft high, with 6 to 8 stems on each plant. Pkt., 25c; 3 pkts., 65c.

BABY'S BREATH
(Gypsophila)

4394 Elegans Grandiflora. Universally popular bell-shaped annual flowers, prized for interspersing among other flowers in bouquets and floral arrangements. Grows easily in any soil and blooms quickly. Finest florist's grade blend of pinks and whites, pkt., 15c; 3 pkts., 35c.

BABY BLUE EYES
(Nemophila)

1470 Brilliant little blue flowers 6 in. across with white centers and very attractive foliage. Originally native to California, it is easily grown and rivals the Peony as a wild flower adaptable for naturalizing, potting, or window boxes. Pkt., 10c; 3 pkts., 25c.

1101—Calendula. Pkt., 10c

1232—Cosmos, Orange Flare. Pkt., 15c

4445—Larkspur, Rosamond. Pkt., 20c

BACHELOR'S BUTTON
(Gomphrena)

1160 Clover-like flowers of strawy texture about ¾ in across. Bloom during mid-summer until frost. They are excellent for borders, cutting, and may be dried out and hung indoors during the winter. Finest mixture, pkt., 15c; 3 pkts., 35c.

BALSAM (Lady Slipper)

4116 Camellia-Flowered, Mixed. Old-fashioned favorites which were always considered indispensable to every garden. Now, through the genius of the hybridizers, the earlier gardeners would gasp with admiration at the vast improvement of the modern varieties. The annual plants have perfectly formed, symmetrical bushes 2 to 3 ft. high, with fine double blooms 2½ in. in diameter. The colors range from intense fiery scarlet, through deep pinks to the more delicate flesh-pinks and chamois-rose, to white, yellow, and violet. The plants prefer good soil in a half-shaded location. They bloom from early summer until frost. Balanced blend of all shades, pkt., 10c; 3 pkts., 25c.

CALENDULA

1100 Orange King. To the plant breeders the gardener owes a debt of gratitude for the remarkable improvements wrought upon the old-time Calendula. The modern versions of the same flower are extra large and double entirely to the center. The variety Orange King is one of the largest, showiest, and brilliant orange flowers of the family. Extra select, dark centered, pkt., 15c; 3 pkts., 35c.

1101 Finest Double Mixture. A choice blend. Pkt., 10c; 3 pkts., 25c.

CALLIOPSIS

1110 One of the showiest and most decorative annual flowers which blooms steadily from early summer until frost. It is very easily grown, thriving in any location and soil. Flowers provide a brilliant range of colors; the foliage is pleasingly feathery. Well suited for beds, borders, or cut flowers. Bicolor tall single mixed. Pkt., 10c; 3 pkts., 25c.

CAMPANULA
(Canterbury Bell)

993 (Annual.) A new annual flower which is becoming more and more popular with gardeners everywhere for beds and borders. The plant grows 2 to 2½ ft. high, each with 6 to 8 flower spikes bearing the familiar bell flowers. This strain is outstanding in that it blooms from seed in less than 6 mo. after sowing. The prize-winning blend offered here won the Gold Medal Award in the 1933 All-America Selections, and has maintained its superiority over competition ever since.

Gold Medal Mixture. Deep rose, Cambridge and violet-blue, pink and white. Pkts., only 10c; 3 pkts., 25c.

CARDINAL CLIMBER
(Ipomea Quamoclit)

4199 Cypress Vine. A graceful rapid-growing annual vine with cardinal-red star-shaped flowers measuring 1 to 1½ inches across. The foliage is sparse, feathery, and glossy, deep green. Vines climb 15 ft. in a season, and carry flowers during the entire summer until frost. Pkt., 10c; 3 for 25c.

CHRYSANTHEMUM

1182 Coronarium, Double Mixed. Dainty button-shaped, double flowers measuring 1½ inches across. The annual blooms range in color from golden yellow to lemon and white, and are carried on splendidly firm stems 18 in. tall, admirably suited for cutting. Fine mixture, pkt., 15c; 3 pkts., 35c.

COSMOS

1232 Early Klondyke Orange Flare. Attractive summer and fall - blooming flowers indispensable to the complete garden. The well-branched stems which carry many showy deep golden orange flowers are excellent for cutting. An easily grown annual that flowers 3 months after sowing. Grows 3 ft. high but does not require staking. Pkt., 15c; 3 pkts., 35c.

1233 Cosmos, Early Sensation. Mammoth flowers 4 to 6 in. across within 10 weeks after sowing. Daintily fluted flowers are carried in profusion on 4- to 6-ft. stems admirably suited for cutting. Finest mixture of pinks and whites. Pkt., 15c; 3 pkts., 35c.

GAILLARDIA (Blanket Flower)

4362 Indian Chief. A most reliable and fast growing annual plant which will withstand great heat and dryness. The flowers grow profusely and are very large, single, and rich bronzy red. They bloom throughout the summer and fall. The long stems, 18 in. tall, make this flower adaptable to bedding arrangements and cutting. Grows well in any good soil in full sunlight. Pkt., 10c; 3 pkts., 25c.

GODETIA

1335 Kelvedon Glory. (New upright single annual.) A newly introduced color in Godetia which will probably do much to increase the popularity of this species. The plant is vigorous and literally covered with deep glowing salmon blossoms. Pkt., 20c; 3 pkts., 50c.

LARKSPUR

1263 Tall Double Stock-Flowered. A fine annual plant which has always enjoyed great popularity but is now even more attractive thanks to the improvements wrought by the breeders. The flowers are now more fully double, larger in size, have better growing habits and present a wider range of more glorious colors than ever before. The stately plants grow 4 ft. high and are well branched. Glorious blend of blues (including azure) violet, white, orchid, rose, lilac, and others. Pkt., 15c; 3 pkts., 35c.

4445 Rosamond. (Tall branching double stock-flowered.) A pure deep rose flower that received the Gold Medal in the 1934 All-America Selections. Pkt., 20c; 3 pkts., 50c.

flowerfield bulb farm

LINARIA (Miniature Snapdragon)

1385 MAROCCANA FAIRY BOUQUET. Very charming, free-flowering border plant in bright and pastel shades of pink, rose, carmine, red, yellow, white, lavender, and violet. Dainty flowers 8 in. high, perfect for the rock garden or border. Pkt., 15c; 3 pkts., 35c.

LOBELIA

1392 BEDDING QUEEN (Pumila Splendens). A most beautiful and satisfactory annual border plant resplendent with dark navy blue flowers throughout the season. The contrasting clear white eye is most attractive. Height 4 inches. Pkt., 20c; 3 pkts., 50c.

LUPINS

1421 ANNUAL MIXED. (The New Hartwegi Giants). A marvelously improved strain of this delightful annual flower in glorious mixed colors of whites and blues. The plant grows 3 to 4 ft. tall and branches close to the ground, developing 4 to 6 flower spikes, each spike producing 25 to 50 blooms. A marvelous garden variety in excellent mixture. Pkt., 10c; 3 pkts., 25c.

MARIGOLD

4494 COLLARETTE CROWN OF GOLD. Odorless. One of the most publicized flowers of 1938, a gold medal winner in the All-America Selections competition for 1937. It was selected due to the fact that it bears no trace of the characteristic Marigold odor in the foliage, stems, or flower. It is a medium sized flower measuring about 2½ inches in diameter., It has a glorious golden orange color with a full crested center of small tubular petals, with long crested cutting stems. Pkt., 15c; 3 for 35c.

4487 YELLOW SUPREME. A creamy yellow carnation-flowered sort with long stems for cutting. Gold Medal Winner 1939 A. A. S. Pkt., 10c; 3 for 25c.

1430 TALL DOUBLE AFRICAN. Large spherical double blooms on 3-ft. stems. An excellent annual for beds, borders, or cutting. Finest mixture. Pkt., 15c; 3 pkts., 35c.

5001 SUNRISE. A marvelous new strain of Marigold discovered in Canada by Mr. W. H. Gale and subsequently developed by the company he represents. The flowers are large and ball-shaped, ingeniously composed of dozens of tiny 5-petaled florets, gracefully interlocking and daintily fringed in effect. The color is brilliant golden yellow, a dazzling pure beauty. They are 100 per cent fully double and commence to bloom around August 15th. (See illustration below.) Pkt., 25c; 3 for 65c.

MARIGOLD—Continued

4490 FRENCH, DWARF DOUBLE-HARMONY. Without question this is one of the very finest Marigolds ever introduced. It is in all respects outstanding. The flowers are charming and distinct, Scabiosa-like in formation with tubular deep orange center petals flanked by broad velvety dark maroon-brown guard petals. The plants are dwarf, about a foot high, compact; exceedingly free blooming and extremely early, coming into flower during the first part of June. Harmony, being 100 per cent true to type, color, and habit, is excellent for use in the garden, either in beds or borders, and most attractive when used for cutting. Pkt., 10c; 3 for 25c.

4491 FRENCH, DWARF DOUBLE MIXED. The finest blend of named varieties and best colors of this strain. All large, perfectly shaped flowers. Pkt., 10c; 3 for 25c.

SPECIAL COLLECTION OF MARIGOLDS

One packet of each of the six Marigolds listed, including the New Marigold Sunrise. Six packets, one each of Sunrise, Crown of Gold, Yellow Supreme, Double African Blend, Dwarf Double Harmony, and Dwarf Double Mixed. Purchased individually would cost 85c. Special at only 60c.

MORNING GLORY
(Ipomoea)

4519 HEAVENLY BLUE (Clarke). Unchallenged as one of the most heavenly shades of blue produced in any flower. It shades delicately towards its golden throat. The flowers are very large and formed characteristically. The morning beauty of the blooms has never been equaled. It is a climber over a fence or small building. Pkt., 15c; 3 for 35c.

TWO EXCEPTIONAL MORNING GLORIES

One pkt. Heavenly Blue, regular price 15c.
One pkt. Scarlett O'Hara, regular price 25c.
Both pkts., when ordered together, 30c.

MORNING GLORY, SCARLETT O'HARA

Gold Medal 1939, A. A. S.

4524. The sensational introduction for this year. Scarlett O'Hara is an entirely new color break in this popular garden flower, a rich dark wine-red or deep rosy crimson. The flowers measure about 4 inches in diameter and are freely produced on fast-growing vines which start blooming within 65 days after the seed is sown. The dark green foliage does not make a heavy growth, giving the plants a very graceful appearance, especially when covering arbors and trellises. (See illustration on page 32.) Pkt., 25c; 3 for 65c.

5001—Marigold, Sunrise. Pkt., 25c

4491—Marigold, Dwarf French. Pkt., 10c

4519—Morning Glory, Heavenly Blue Pkt., 15c

flowerfield, long island, New York

NASTURTIUM (Lobb's)

1460 TRAILING AND TALL VARIETIES. A well-balanced mixture of these free blooming Nasturtiums, which grow very easily under the most varied climatic and soil conditions. Pkt., 10c; 3 for 25c; 6 for 40c.

NASTURTIUM, DWARF

1461 SWEET SCENTED. A Gem mixture of dwarf gemlike plants with an excellent color range. Pkt., 10c; 3 for.25c; 6 for 40c.

PETUNIA
Balcony (Hybrida Pendula)

This showy strain bears flowers 3 inches in diameter from early summer until frost. It is particularly suited for window boxes.
556 Red.
1493 Blue.
744 Mixture of Reds, Blues, and other hues.
Any of the above: 15c per pkt.; 3 for 35c.

2103 SINGLE FRINGED, DAINTY LADY (Grandiflora). Twice a winner of merit in 1935 and 1936 selections. This fringed-edge Petunia is highly popular among gardeners. The compact blooms are beautifully luminous, in a light lemon-yellow hue. Pkt., 25c; 3 for 65c.

Hybrida, Spreading Bedding

2143 FLAMING VELVET. This superb flower received the Gold Medal Award in the 1936 All-America Selections. The plants are literally weighed down with the velvety blood-red blossoms, which possess a remarkable and attractive luminous glow. Pkt., 25c; 3 for 65c.

4572 GRANDIFLORA, BURGUNDY. A marvelous contribution to the flower world, this variety was the Silver Medal winner in the 1937 All-America Selections. As its name implies, the flowers are colored a rich wine-red and are embellished which a contrasting white throat. Pkt., 30c; 3 for 50c.

4587 RUFFLED GIANTS. Ruffled monsters, a half dwarf type of erect and robust habit. The flowers are very large and ruffled with open shallow throats. The colors are mostly of the red and desirable dark shades richly marked and veined. Glamorous beauties. Pkt., 35c; 3 for 90c.

4599 GRANDIFLORA, FLUFFY RUFFLES. Single fringed. A gorgeous mixture of light shades finely fringed and ruffled. A magnificent variety of color. Pkt., 30c; 3 for 80c.

5002 RUFFLED GIANT, MARILYN. This ruffled Giant type of Petunia has much greater individual beauty than many other varieties, and because the popularity of salmon-colored garden flowers is unquestioned, Petunia Marilyn should be one of the leading selections for this season. Ruffled flowers but not fringed, 4 to 5 inches diameter, in a glowing shade of salmon-rose strongly veined a deeper salmon-rose. The over-all salmon color blends delicately lighter toward its ruffled edges. Unquestionably one of the most attractively colored of any Petunia. Pkt., 35c; 3 for 90c.

BLUE RIBBON COMBINATION PETUNIA PACKET

One packet of each of the following prize Petunias: Balcony Blend, Dainty Lady, Flaming Velvet, Burgundy, Ruffled Giant, Fluffy Ruffles, and the New Ruffled Giant Marilyn.
Seven packets, which would cost $1.85 if purchased individually, offered for only $1.25.

PHLOX DRUMMONDI
Grandiflora

An excellent new strain with flowers more than an inch in diameter. Lovely pastel shades range from appleblossom, pink, rose, light blue, and mauve; each bloom having an attractive creamy white eye. Award of Merit in 1935 All-America Selections.
4604 LAVENDER.
4605 PINK.
4606 ISABELLINA. Pale primrose, buff.
4607 SCARLET.
4608 GIGANTEA ART SHADES, The blend of the best named varieties, including the shades above and many others.
Any of the above: 15c per pkt.; 3 for 35c.

PHLOX DRUMMONDI GARDEN
One of each of the 5 above pkts., 50c.

SALVIA SPLENDENS
Or Scarlet Sage

4695 BONFIRE or CLARA BEDMAN. A most brilliant bedding plant that carries blooms from early summer until late fall. The dark green dense-foliaged plants are globular and erect, and fully produce their scarlet-red flowers. An annual flower that does best when the seeds are started early indoors in boxes. Pkt., 15c; 3 for 35c.

SALPIGLOSSIS (Painted Tongue)

1565 Very fine trumpet-shaped annual flowers resembling the Gloxinias in appearance. Blossoms are large and of a velvety texture, with gold, yellow, crimson, and purple. Plants grow 2 feet high, and are best when spaced 1 foot apart. Finest blend of all colors, large flowering. Pkt., 10c; 3 pkts., 25c.

SCABIOSA
Double Tall and Large Flowered

4705 An amazing development of the old-fashioned Pincushion flower or Mourning Bride. The pincushion effect caused by the stamens sticking out so that they resemble pins stuck into a cushion has been eliminated. The improved flower has complete doubleness which entirely eliminates the Pincushion center, and has become one of the most popular and easily grown annuals. It grows 3 feet tall in rich colors with firm stems that cut extremely well. A marvelous mixture of all colors. Pkt., 10c; 3 for 25c.

2338 IMPERIAL GIANTS, BLUE MOON. Hybridists in their unending quest for new flowers are ofttimes astounded by the unsuspected and unimagined beauty they have succeeded in producing by their plant guidance and care. This glorious achievement was accomplished by the very excellent hybridizing technique practiced by Bodger, who has introduced this magnificent flower. Instead of flowers composed of a few rows of broad petals surmounted by a flat pincushion-like top of small petals, this new introduction has flowers composed entirely of broad, heavy, wavy petals, eliminating the pincushion center entirely. In other words, the flower is literally fully double. They are extremely large, 2¾ inches across and 2 to 2¾ inches deep, about the shape of an old-fashioned beehive. The color is a rich deep lavender-blue, a shade which maintains the effectiveness indoors and out. The plant is upright, 42 to 48 inches in height. Its stems are strong and wiry, and hold the flowers proudly erect. It is ideal for cutting because of its long 27-inch stems. (See illustration on page 32.) Pkt., 25c; 3 for 65c.

SCHIZANTHUS
(Butterfly Flower)

1600 SUNSET HYBRIDS. Large butterfly-shaped flowers brilliantly colored in bright reds and carmine shades with delicate gold markings. The foliage is gracefully fernlike, the plants robust and bushy. A favorite of the discriminating flower fancier. Pkt., 15c; 3 for 35c.

STOCKS

4757 DOUBLE LARGE FLOWERING TEN WEEK (Gilliflower). A lovely mixture of named varieties. These fragrant flowers that appear like small rosettes in a wide range of distinct soft shades are fine for bedding. They do well in a well-limed soil in a cool location. Pkt., 10c; 3 for 25c.

STRAWFLOWER (Helichrysum)

4403 MONSTROSUM. A large-flowering annual with double brightly colored blooms. Very effective for beds and borders as the blooms remain during summer and fall. Grows about 30 inches high. The colors range from canary-yellow, golden, scarlet, crimson, and rose, to silvery pink, silver and violet. The best named varieties have been used in making up this fine blend. Pkt., 10c; 3 for 25c.

SWEET PEAS

4803 GRANDIFLORA. One of the well-balanced mixtures of this very desirable garden species. Pkt., 20c; 3 for 50c.
4802 SPENCER SWEET PEAS. Early flowering. An extra choice mixture well balanced with the newest and brightest colors. A magnificent collection. Pkt., 20c; 3 for 50c.

4817 SPENCER SWEET PEAS. Late flowering. An unrivaled mixture containing the finest selection of the most attractive named varieties including the newest novelties. Pkt., 20c; 3 for 50c.

VERBENA (Gigantea)

1745 FLORADALE BEAUTY. 1937 Award of Merit. Multicolored, miniature annual plant which is perfect for borders, bedding, rock gardens, window boxes, and cutting. The individual florets are 1½ inches across, and form large trusses 4 to 5 inches in diameter which bloom during the latter part of summer and fall. This strain won the 1937 Award of Merit in the All-America Selections for the all-around excellence and brilliance of its flower masses of rosy red and bright rose-pink. Pkt., 25c; 3 pkts., 65c.

ZINNIA
Gold Medal Dahlia-Flowered

The Dahlia-Flowered Strain introduced by Bodger, one of the world's leading seed growers, has steadily gained in popularity since the time of its origination. The very robust plants are of medium height, 2½ to 3 feet, and bear many strong stems of fully double, huge flowers which resemble the Show type of Dahlia.

2269 CANARY BIRD. Rich canary-yellow.
2270 POLAR BEAR. Large creamy white.
2274 EXQUISITE. Light rose, deep rose center.
2275 CRIMSON MONARCH. Deep crimson, flowers are very large.
2277 PURPLE PRINCE. Deep purple.
Any of the above: 15c per pkt.; 3 for 35c.
Collection of Gold Medal Flowered Zinnias: One each of the above selected varieties, 5 pkts. for 50c.
4916 DAHLIA-FLOWERING MIXTURE. A blend of the finest varieties, those above and many others, all grown as separate colors before being mixed in perfect color proportion. Pkt., 10c; 3 for 25c.

Baby, Pompon or Lilliput Types— New Pastels

The petite Lilliputs are among the most popular Zinnias for cut flower use, being especially prized for table decorations. The flowers are small, compact, and symmetrical, on strong-stemmed, 12- to 15-inch plants. Very free and early flowering, blooming 45 days after sowing.

2034 ROSEBUD. Rose-pink.
2040 WHITE.
2041 LILAC GEM. Lilac.
Pkt., 20c; 3 for 50c.

Lilliput—New Pastel Mixture

2346 This New Pastel Mixture blends the very lovely soft shades of apricot, peach, creamy-yellow, shell-pink, delicate salmon, light rose, and orchid; all of which are outstanding favorites with florists and cut flower growers. Pkt., 20c; 3 for 50c.

Fantasy

5003 WHITE LIGHT. Recommended 1938 A. A. S. Again hybridizer Bodger triumphed with their Fantasy Zinnias and received for the third time, recognition in the All-America Selections with their new introduction, White Light, which is considered a very worthy successor to Star Dust and The Mixture, both of which were granted Awards of Merit at the time of their introduction. The color is nearest to white of any Zinnia yet developed. It is medium sized, shaggy petaled, a pure restful little beauty, lovely in vases or in the garden. It lends a soft note of restfulness to any location selected for it. Pkt., 25c; 3 for 65c.

flowerfield bulb farm

4599—Petunia, Fluffy Ruffles. (A.) Pkt., 30c

4916—Dahlia-Flowered Zinnias. (A.) Pkt., 10c

1461—Dwarf Nasturtium. (A.) Pkt., 10c

Flowerfield Perennial Garden

Glorious flowers may be yours for years to come by planting perennials. The varieties listed below include those which are most reliable
and easily grown, and some of them will bloom in the first year if sown
early in spring under favorable conditions. In the vicinity of New
York City they may be sown during very early spring, until the first
part of August.

1260—Delphinium. (P.) Pkt., 20c

flowerfield, long island, New York

Special Selection
of 11 Perennials

Would cost $1.60 if purchased by individual packets. When
ordered together the price is only $1.00 for the entire

PERENNIAL COLLECTION

4036 ALYSSUM, Gold Dust.
2200 CAMPANULA (Canterbury Bells). Single varieties.
4268 COLUMBINE (Aquilegia.) Improved varieties.
1220 COREOPSIS GRANDIFLORA, California Sunbeam.
2129 DIANTHUS. Rock garden pinks.
4342 FORGET-ME-NOTS. Blue.
2243 GEUM, Mrs. Bradshaw.
1360 HOLLYHOCK, Double Triumph Mixture.
1420 LUPINS. Perennial.
2090 SWEET WILLIAM. Double.
1755 VIOLA (Tufted Pansies).

Value $1.60 If Purchased Individually.

Only $1.00 for 11 Perennials

Flowerfield Perennial Flower Seeds

In contradistinction to the annuals, which bloom and die within the first summer season, the perennials live for many years after they are sown. A few of the varieties, if sown very early, will flower during the first year, although two years are usually required for blooms to appear. The plants, when matured, flower each year, and die down to the roots in late fall. The roots remain dormant until the following spring when they again send up strong shoots which subsequently burst forth with brilliant color.

ALYSSUM

4036 Saxatile, Gold Dust. A perfectly hardy member of the Alyssum family. The dwarf plants, which grow 9 to 12 inches high, thrive well in poor dry soil and sunny locations. The brilliant golden yellow flowers bloom so profusely that they completely hide the plant stems and foliage. It is especially suited to the rock garden and for edgings. Pkt., 15c; 3 pkts., 35c.

CAMPANULA

994 Hardy Canterbury Bells (Cup-and-Saucer). Showy bell-like flowers with an unusually large calyx which gives the effect of a miniature cup and saucer. The plants bloom in June and grow about 2 to 2½ ft. high. This choicest mixture includes the finest blues, rose, and white. Pkt., 10c; three for 25c.

2200 Hardy Canterbury Bells, Single Varieties. A fine blend of the most interesting and colorful single varieties. Pkt., 10c; 3 pkts., 25c.

COLUMBINE (Aquilegia)

4268 Improved Varieties. Lovely perennial which blooms in the spring. It possesses an unusual airy appearance which makes it a graceful and desirable addition to the border. It is also well suited for cutting. A sunny or half-shaded location in a well-drained semi-rich soil is best. Long-spurred improved varieties, including all richest colors. Pkt., 20c; 3 pkts., 50c.

COREOPSIS GRANDIFLORA

1220 Lanceolata (California Sunbeam). An old-time favorite hardy perennial flower. Much of its popularity arises from its ease of culture and profusion of blooms. Flowers are large and showy, and of bright yellow color, blooming from June till late fall. Height 30 inches. Pkt., 10c; 3 pkts., 25c.

DELPHINIUM
(Perennial Larkspur)

1260 Gold-Medal Hybrids. One of the most popular and magnificent of all the perennials for showy garden displays and cutting. The massive, colored spikes rise 3 to 4 feet. They are easily grown and will bloom during the first year if planted in deep, rich, well-drained soil. Choice mixture of many beautiful shades. Pkt., 20c; 3 pkts., 50c.

DIANTHUS

2129 Rock Garden Pinks (Cruentus). Very dark crimson flowers, borne in clusters, which make them ideal for borders as well as the rock garden. The plants grow about 2 ft. high. Pkt., 20c; 3 pkts., 50c.

FORGET-ME-NOT (Myosotis)

4342 Alpestris. Blue. A biennial well suited to rock gardens and which will bloom early in spring. The seed may be sown from spring till mid-summer and fine showy masses of blue on plants 1 ft. high will be in bloom. Pkt., 10c; 3 pkts., 25c.

GEUM

2243 Mrs. Bradshaw. Delicate double-flowered plants which are hardy if given protection during the winter. The brilliant scarlet flowers bloom from June to September. Pkt., 15c; 3 pkts., 35c.

HOLLYHOCK (Althea Rosea)

1360 Double Triumph Mixture. Beautifully fringed rosette flowers of this majestic perennial in a diversity of new shades and bi-color combinations, growing 5 to 7 ft. high. They are excellent when planted in a line as a background. Superb blend of colors. Pkt., 15c; 3 pkts., 35c.

LUPINS

1420 Polyphyllus. Beautiful free-blooming plants, well suited for cutting, which bloom during May and June. The tall stately spikes grow 3 ft. high and proudly carry racemes of blue, rose, and white blossoms. Blend of colors, pkt., 10c; 3 pkts., 25c.

PANSY

1480 Giants of California. One of the old standbys and popular garden favorites. When planted in a sunny position in good, rich and moist soil, they will thrive beautifully, producing strong, bushy plants. They may be planted in early spring, for summer blooming, or in early fall to provide spring flowers. Special mixture of giant types. Pkt., 25c; 3 pkts., 65c.

POPPY NUDICAULE
(Iceland Poppy)

1518 Roseum, Coonara Pinks. A glorious new strain of Iceland Poppies, those popular hardy perennials which bloom during the first season almost as quickly as do the annuals. Of graceful and dainty habit, the brilliantly pink shaded flowers nod in great profusion above the bright green fernlike foliage. Fine mixture of light shades, large flowers. Pkt., 20c; 3 pkts., 50c.

PYRETHRUM
(Chrysanthemum)

999 Roseum. Unusual flowers with fern-like leaves, which enhance the beauty of the plant even when not in bloom. This strain is of easy culture, and will bloom twice in one summer season if cut back in the spring. An exceptional "florists grade" of white, rose, pink, crimson, and red. Pkt., 20c; 3 pkts., 50c.

SWEET WILLIAM

2090 Double. Garden favorite since time immemorial, these perennial plants carry, during May and June, showy flower-heads made up of many individual blooms. They are very easy to grow, and usually attain a height of 1 to 1½ ft. Finest selected mixture. Pkt., 10c; 3 pkts., 25c.

VIOLA (Tufted Pansies)

1755. Perennial flowers resembling miniature pansies in appearance. They make a fine display in beds, edgings, and rockeries. The colors range from deep violet, purple, blues, pinks, and reds to clear white. Finest cornuta blend. Pkt., 25c; 3 pkts., 65c.

Dependable Lawn Grass Mixtures
Recommended by Flowerfield

After patient investigation and careful comparison of the analysis of various LAWN GRASS SEED offered today, we decided to offer to our customers the very best quality LAWN GRASS SEED mixtures that could be obtained.

In our effort to measure the quality of the LAWN GRASS SEED, we disregarded the cost of the product, so that our selection would in no way be prejudiced in that direction. We then demanded that mixtures be prepared so that our customers could choose from a few special mixtures, each adapt-

able to the specific conditions under which the seed was to be sown; our final and most important requisite was, that each container or bag in which the seed was packed must have attached to it the analysis of the particular mixture it contained.

We now offer a LAWN GRASS SEED, which in our opinion is the very best seed obtainable, and which we believe has met the rigid qualifying specifications we established. It is the product of one of the most reliable and very best known producers of LAWN GRASS SEED.

TURF-MAKER
A Superb Mixture

Not a secret formula, but a different one made up primarily of Kentucky Blue Grass and Colonial Bent with Fancy Red Top and Poa trivialis as "nurses". It is so blended that it will produce lasting, fine-textured turf east of the Mississippi and almost anywhere north of the Mason-Dixon line. This mixture is 90% perennial and over 97% pure seed. The complete analysis of this superb mixture appears on every package.

1-lb. can	$ 0.65
3-lb. bag	1.90
5-lb. bag	3.00
10-lb. bag	5.75
100-lb. bag	50.00

TURF-MAKER
for Poor Soils

No. 170 was designed for a specific job on very sandy soils on Long Island. The phenomenal results obtained prompted us to offer it to those who cannot or do not care to improve their soil to grow "regular" mixtures. No. 170 is slow to mature, and best results are obtained when seeding is accomplished in early September. If spring seeding is necessary, we recommend that be sown early.

1-lb. can	$ 1.00
3-lb. bag	2.60
5-lb. bag	4.75
10-lb. bag	8.25
100-lb. bag	75.00

TRUE-SHADE
for Shady Spots

An excellent Shady Mixture. Fine textured and deep-rooting, it blends well with Turf-Maker so that uniform turf extends well under quite dense shade. This mixture includes Chewings Fescue, Poa trivialis, and Kentucky Blue Grass with the balance recleaned Red Top, 97% pure seed.

1 lb.	$ 0.75
3-lb. bag	2.15
5-lb. bag	3.50
10-lb. bag	6.75
100-lb. bag	60.00

CENTRAL STATES
for General Homes

A formula for general home use. 10% is heavy, recleaned Kentucky Blue Grass with the balance Fancy Red Top, White Clover and Pacey's Rye Grass. Use of these refined grasses permits the low inert content of less than 10% and the weed content is at a minimum.

1-lb.	$ 0.50
3-lb. bag	1.45
5-lb. bag	2.25
10-lb. bag	4.25
100-lb. bag	35.00

INDIVIDUAL GRASSES

	Lb.
WHITE CLOVER, Woodco Brand	$0.65
KENTISH WILD WHITE CLOVER	2.00
SEASIDE BENT (Certified Blue Tag)	1.50

	Lb.
COLONIAL BENT (Certified Blue Tag)	$1.50
EMERALD VELVET BENT	5.50
PIPER VELVET BENT (B.P.I. 14276)	7.50

PIPER BENT STOLONS, $1.00 per square foot of sod.

flowerfield bulb farm

Flowerfield's Northern Grown Cannas

City of Portland
Deep rich pink. Green foliage. Height 5 feet.

Orange Bedder
Bright orange with some scarlet suffusion. Green foliage. Height 4 to 5 feet.

The President
The outstanding red Canna, having immense trusses of fiery red flowers, produced in great profusion. A vigorous plant, with green foliage. Height 5 feet.

Complete list of Cannas on page 22.

SPECIAL OFFERING
of CANNAS

Cannas for an attractive bed or border. Strong roots that will give excellent results.

10 each of the following (50 roots) **$5**.50   **5** each of the following (25 roots) **$3**.00

Red. Bronze foliage.
Red. Green foliage.
Pink. Green foliage.
Yellow. Green foliage.
Yellow. Red blotch—green foliage.

The President

Orange Bedder

City of Portland

[40]

Lightning Source UK Ltd.
Milton Keynes UK
UKHW020023181218
334174UK00013B/2106/P